CARTOMANCY *with the*
LENORMAND
and the TAROT

About the Author

Patrick Dunn has studied witchcraft, the Qabalah, chaos magic, and anything else he can get his hands on. In addition to obtaining his PhD in literature, he has studied linguistics and stylistics. He lives in Illinois, where he teaches English Literature. Dunn is also the author of *Postmodern Magic: The Art of Magic in the Information Age.*

To Write to the Author

If you wish to contact the author or would like more information about this book, please write to the author in care of Llewellyn Worldwide Ltd. and we will forward your request. Both the author and publisher appreciate hearing from you and learning of your enjoyment of this book and how it has helped you. Llewellyn Worldwide Ltd. cannot guarantee that every letter written to the author can be answered, but all will be forwarded. Please write to:

Patrick Dunn
℅ Llewellyn Worldwide
2143 Wooddale Drive Dept. 978-0-7387-3600-6
Woodbury, MN 55125-2989
Please enclose a self-addressed stamped envelope for reply,
or $1.00 to cover costs. If outside the U.S.A., enclose
an international postal reply coupon.

Many of Llewellyn's authors have websites with additional information and resources. For more information, please visit our website at http://www.llewellyn.com

PATRICK DUNN

CARTOMANCY *with the* LENORMAND *and the* TAROT

Create Meaning & Gain Insight from the Cards

Llewellyn Publications
Woodbury, Minnesota

FIRST EDITION
First Printing, 2013

Cover art © 2013
        Vintage paper scroll © iStockphoto.com/Alexander Novikov
Cover design by Kevin R. Brown
Editing by Laura Graves
Interior illustrations © Llewellyn Art Department except Robert Fludd's Mirror of the Whole of Nature © Image file courtesy of Liam Quinn: www.fromoidbooks.org
Interior tarot card art (reprinted by permission):
Lo Scarabeo: Universal Tarot © Roberto DeAngelis
        French Cartomancy Tarot © Madame Lenormand & Laura Tuan

Llewellyn is a registered trademark of Llewellyn Worldwide Ltd.

Library of Congress Cataloging-in-Publication Data
Dunn, Patrick, 1975-
   Cartomancy with the Lenormand and the tarot : create meaning & gain insight from the cards / Patrick Dunn. — First edition.
       p. cm.
   Includes bibliographical references and index.
   ISBN 978-0-7387-3600-6
1. Tarot. 2. Le Normand, M. A. (Marie-Anne Ad?laide), 1772-1843—Miscellanea. I. Title.
   BF1879.T2D86 2013
   133.3'2424—dc23
                                                              2013009838

Llewellyn Publications
A Division of Llewellyn Worldwide Ltd.
2143 Wooddale Drive
Woodbury, MN 55125-2989
www.llewellyn.com

Printed in the United States of America

To my mother,
Joyce,
who taught me the tarot
and so much more

Contents

Chapter X   The Grammar of Symbols   129

Chapter XI   Intuitive Reading   141

Chapter XII   Collaborative Reading   153

Chapter XIII   Symbolic Interaction Between
                 the Lenormand and Tarot   161

Chapter XIV   Synergy   179

Chapter XV   DIY   193

Chapter XVI   Divination and Magic   207

Epilogue   Keys of Cardboard   223

Appendix I   Okay, Fine, A List of Meanings for the Cards,
                 if You Insist   225

Appendix II   Lenormand Keyword Table   249

                 Bibliography   255

                 Index   259

Acknowledgments

I'm always tempted to simply list everyone I know in acknowledgments, because I am blessed with so many wonderful friends, neighbors, and colleagues in every part of my life. I will limit myself, however, to just a few, with no implication that others are not also worthy of thanks for their help and support, witting and unwitting.

I wish to thank Richard, for his encouragement and patience with my writerly quirks.

Thanks also to my friends Chris, Ryan, Peter, and Eric, all of whom have shaped my thoughts through discussion, debate, and the best kind of academic argument. Thanks to Chris again, for reading an early draft of this book and offering his usual helpful feedback.

Thanks also to the Aeclectic Tarot forums, where the community of Lenormand readers are more than willing to share their techniques and ideas.

I also thank the Kindred Spirits Intuitive Arts Center in Oswego, IL, for hosting me on several occasions as a guest and showing interest in my work.

Mary K. Greer offered honest, helpful, and knowledgeable criticism of an earlier version of this book, and for that and the improvement it made to the book, I'm very grateful.

Elysia Gallo, my editor at Llewellyn, has been a great help. Editors do a lot more than mark apostrophe errors. Without good editors, books would never see the light of day, and Llewellyn has some of the best editors in publishing. I am grateful for her assistance, her spot-on suggestions, and her patience with those same aforementioned writerly quirks.

If I've missed anyone, I hope they will not take it as a sign of ingratitude, instead of the honest mistake that it is. And, of course, there are helpers invisible to sensate eyes whom I also must thank, but I'll refrain from listing their names here.

ὁ ἄναξ οὗ τὸ μαντεῖόν ἐστι τὸ ἐν Δελφοῖς οὔτε λέγει οὔτε
κρύπτει ἀλλὰ σημαίνει
—Heraclitus, frag. 93

The Lord whose oracle is at Delphi
neither speaks clearly nor conceals, but signifies.

Introduction

O n the surface, this book is about cartomancy, the art of divination through the use of cards. I focus on two particular decks: the tarot and the Lenormand, decks of divination cards based on playing cards. I wanted to approach the Lenormand this way because it is little-known in the United States, but the tarot is familiar to many people. I wanted to use the tarot as a gateway into the Lenormand, which I have found a rewarding system in its own right. At the same time, I wished to say some modestly new things about the tarot and to provide some ways to use the two systems together that have proven useful to me personally. The universal symbolism of the Lenormand, so accessible and simple, can shine a clear light on the tarot, and the complex cosmology and philosophy of the tarot can lend depth and meaning to the Lenormand. That is one level of what I am trying to accomplish with this book.

Read at another level, this is a book about types of knowledge and ways of listening. The idea that random pieces of cardboard can tell the future seems absurd. And yet, after years of experimenting, I conclude that they can at least forecast (if not predict) with as much accuracy as the meteorologist. So this book serves as a meditation on the strangeness of that worldview and the wonder of it.

The traditional approach to the Lenormand is to lay out a list of meanings for the cards, both singly and in combination with each other. Different countries—and, to be honest, different readers—all have slight differences in what particular cards mean, and some readers will even argue about the "right" meaning of a card. This traditional approach is not my own. I respect it as an approach, and I certainly respect the tradition. But tradition is not monolithic; it is not an unchanging monument that we must just salute. I approach the cards with a more postmodern spirit, seeing them as a collection of symbols that gain meaning in their relationships to each other but also in their relationships to those who use them. A simple list of meanings, while useful for some, is not this book's goal. I respect and honor the traditions of Lenormand reading, but this is not an entirely traditional book.

Similarly, this book is only secondarily a how-to book. You can learn to read the Lenormand, and to some extent, the tarot from it, but I am assuming some knowledge of tarot and a willingness to work with the Lenormand. This is not just a book about how to lay out Lenormand cards and read them; it is a book about how to develop a relationship with these fascinating cards. And like most relationships, it requires work and care and listening. My method is not, therefore, to prescribe recipes for reading the cards, but to give suggestions for how to approach them and learn to read them organically.

The Skeptical Cartomancer

Believe it or not, I am a skeptic. Such a label might be odd for an author of occult books. But I am a skeptic in the older sense of the word; I find it hard to believe on hearsay alone. I need data—either scientific data or personal experience—to believe a claim is true. Moreover, I always keep in mind the alternate ways of interpreting data: my divinations may be self-delusions, my religious experiences hallucinations, my neighbors figments of my imagination. But in general, as I trust that my neighbors exist (and a good thing, too, since I need to feed their cat tomorrow morning), I also trust that the many startling predictions I have made with the tarot, the Lenormand, and other systems are actual predictions and not just a trick of my self-deluding mind.

At its root, divination is about knowledge. There are two ways to think about knowledge. First, we can imagine that knowledge is a thing that enters our head through observation of the external or physical world: this view of knowledge is called *externalism*. Or we can imagine that we build knowledge in our minds as a response not just to external sensory input but also our previous knowledge, our inner landscape, and perhaps even other unconscious forces. This model of knowledge is called *constructivism*, and it is the model of knowledge I prefer and will assume in this book. The constructivist approach is another way this book differs from the traditional approach to the Lenormand, which is largely externalist.

We build knowledge by linking symbols together in patterns. The more complex the pattern, the more complex the knowledge. Of course, some patterns give us no useful knowledge about the world, but these patterns may have value beyond their usefulness. An artist, for example, creates patterns that don't actually accomplish anything, but are worthwhile as beautiful objects.

A pattern is "useful" when it tells us something about other patterns of symbols we observe: when it predicts how those patterns will fall out or explains their organization. So an equation describing the motions of the planets is useful because it allows us to calculate orbits of objects we experience as external to ourselves. We interpret this kind of knowledge or pattern-making to be "scientific."

A pattern that relates symbols to other symbols is "aesthetic." It pleases some sense of beauty in our own minds, and while it may tell us truths or make predictions, those truths are not observer-independent and those predictions are not unchangeable. Art, music, and poetry create these aesthetic patterns.

Magic—and I include cartomancy in that category—combines these two approaches. Magic erases the line between inner and outer experience, between consciousness and seemingly external matter. So magic offers another way of organizing knowledge, without sacrificing the obvious benefits of scientific thinking. Magic is about thinking flexibly.

Critics of divination sometimes argue that humans detect patterns in random material, and there is no guarantee that such a pattern is "really there." For example, from one angle a rock formation on Mars looks startlingly like a face. The pictures of this formation led to debate about whether or not the formation is an artifact, but later pictures have shown that, from other angles, there is not anything startling about the formation at all. We like to perceive patterns and we notice even patterns that are not really there. We don't even have to look at Mars for examples: we can see a unicorn in the clouds that isn't really there.

But what does that mean, "not really there"? For one thing, the term "pattern" is only meaningful when applied to stuff that we experience. A bunch of stuff doesn't form a pattern until we detect a pattern in it. To detect a pattern is to create one, and so any pattern we detect is really there by definition. There may not be a face on Mars or a unicorn in the clouds, but there is the image of a face and a unicorn once I see one. The existence of a pattern does not necessarily imply an intelligence placed it there, or that it is an artifact, or even that the pattern really means anything. But that we perceive a pattern tells us something about our minds. The face on Mars wasn't made by anyone and doesn't necessarily mean anything about Mars itself, but it does tell us a bit about what we hope to find when we look at other bodies in space: we hope to find ourselves. I think that's a valuable thing to understand, even if it is just our natural tendency to see patterns everywhere.

People do have a tendency to see patterns and experience a sense of meaningfulness. Psychologists call this *apophenia*, which is the perception of meanings in random data. For example, we could say that the names of the constellations come from seeing patterns among them that are not there. An astronomer will tell you that the stars in any given constellation are not even anywhere near each other; they only appear to be related from the viewpoint of those living on Earth. An astronomer will tell you, that contrary to the beliefs of astrologers, in reality, the constellations are meaningless and random.

And yet, astronomers still learn the names and locations of the constellations, although they do not use them the way astrologers do (for one thing, they learn a lot more of them). Although Aries is not the willful and enthusiastic child to an astronomer, the constellation still has meaning for him or her. It's a street sign in the sky to which the astronomer attaches meaning.

This analogy to street signs is quite apt. There's a street in Chicago called Halsted. It's one of my favorite streets: there are several interesting stores, a few quirky places to eat, and if you go north far enough, you end up in one of Chicago's gay neighborhoods. To me, the word *Halsted* might as well as be random syllables, because I have no idea who or what Halsted might have been originally. But I, along with probably a million or so Chicagoans, have ascribed meaning to that name.

When people argue that this tendency to see patterns in random stuff explains away divination, they fail to recognize that meaning does not exist in patterns. Information does. We create meaning only by taking that information and connecting it to other patterns of information. The origin of the original information is mostly irrelevant, whether it be random or ordered. There can indeed be meaning in random information (ask any surrealist artist) and ordered information can lack meaning, because meaning is entirely and completely a matter of perception. To see meaning is to create meaning.

A more useful distinction might be whether or not that meaning is useful. Does it fit with our other experiences to help us understand something in a new way? Or, from an externalist perspective, is it true? Some meanings are not useful: it's probably not useful to argue that the face on Mars represents an artifact. We cannot fit that meaning into a pattern of similar meaning: in other words, we see no other evidence for artifacts on Mars. If we did, perhaps it would be helpful to imagine the face as an artifact. Similarly, if we decide that we can't leave the house because we saw a black cat, the meaning we give to that event isn't particularly useful. It's superstition, not divination.

I'm not arguing that anything goes when it comes to knowledge, and that everything is true. Some claims are false (by which I mean profoundly unusual and incongruent with most people's experiences), and some people are delusional. The scientific method offers a way to weed through many claims about the physical world and evaluate them. But it cannot investigate a lot of questions that matter very much: love, beauty, and meaning. For that we need other systems of knowledge, built out of symbols and shared cultural experiences.

It's easy to dismiss entire areas of human experience as what militant skeptics call "woo-woo." It requires a bit more intellectual courage and rigor to consider every pattern on its own merits. Ultimately, we must rely on experience, because that is all we have. There is no pure reason, and never can be, because our material for reason always comes through our senses. We can create systems of knowledge such as science to help us organize and evaluate meanings, but we must always keep in mind that even our systems of knowledge are invented out of our experiences. If I experience a meaning in a random pattern, I have to evaluate it by comparing it to my other experiences. If I see the tarot card the Magician, I need to think about where there is skill in my experience, and if I see the Lenormand card 2–Clover, I need to find in my experience where luck and simplicity might fit.

I am becoming more and more convinced that divinatory patterns are not always random. While I do not think that science is well suited to investigate magic, there are statistical techniques that can help identify whether a signal is meaningful or not. Essentially, these techniques involve clustering of data. If a seemingly random collection of data—say, a string of letters—contains information, you can expect a sample of that data to repeat itself to a statistically significant degree. For example, in English, if I give you the letter Q and ask you what letter might follow it, you will know that it is very likely to be U. Or if I ask you to complete the sentence "the very happy _____ played with his new toy," you'll probably fill in the blank with "boy," "child," or "puppy," but probably not with "sandwich" or "toaster." You can predict, statistically, what is likely to come next, because language isn't random.

The problem with this kind of analysis of divination is acquiring a good sample of divinations to analyze. Ideally, the sample should be all on the same topic by the same diviner. It'd be tricky to find a reader who reads about the same topics over and over again. Also, the sample—the number of readings—needs to be large enough to be significant. For this kind of analysis, I'd like at least thirty different readings, all on the same topic by the same diviner. The point here is not to dive into the endlessly fascinating world of statistical analysis, but to show how hard it would be to apply those tools to the practice of divination.

On the other hand, a lot of tarot card readers draw a single card for meditation and divination at the beginning of the day. Those readers who record the card they draw create a data set that is uniquely suited to this kind of analysis. Jane English, a scientist who became interested in the tarot, performed a kind of statistical analysis called a "chi-squared" test to investigate whether or not particular readers' daily cards were truly statistically random. What she discovered is that to a very high level of significance, the cards chosen by readers tend to cluster into nonrandom patterns.[1] She took her own readings and analyzed the number of times each card appeared. By chance, you would expect a daily draw to spread out over time, so that cards are more or less evenly represented. What she discovered is that certain cards, ones having to do with her concerns, showed up much more often. When she duplicated the experiment by drawing numbered and meaningless cards, they were distributed randomly.

English's research has not, to my knowledge, been published in a peer-reviewed journal. Nor is it likely to be. As much as I approve of and respect the peer review process and the scientific method, I know very well that research like English's, which calls into question

---

1. Jane English, "A Scientist's Experience with Tarot," *Wheel of the Tarot: A New Revolution,* ed. James Wanless and Angeles Arrien (Carmel, CA: Merrill-West Publishing, 1992), 16–23.

the fundamental preconceptions of science, is unlikely to see peer reviewed publication. One common critique of paranormal research is that it requires much more evidence than other results simply because it does call into question the preconceptions of science. I doubt that even the best constructed experiment or analysis that shows divination works will get much respect from the scientific community for the foreseeable future.

Leaving aside statistical analysis and scientific validation, the real question we have to ask ourselves when we divine is, do I know something I did not know before? If so, the divination is a success. And in order to evaluate that new knowledge, we have to have a firm and unwavering commitment to honest introspection: we must have the courage to look at ourselves.

The epigraph of this book is a fragment of Heraclitus, number 93, in which he says, "The Lord whose oracle is at Delphi neither speaks clearly nor conceals, but signifies." The lord of the oracle at Delphi is Apollo, the god of divination. The meaning of this fragment, like most of the fragments of Heraclitus, isn't entirely obvious, but I've always been intrigued by the amazing degree of sophistication revealed in it. This statement sounds like something a modern scholar of symbols might say about a modern poem, but Heraclitus lived about 500 BCE.

This book isn't just a list of card meanings and spreads, then, but an exploration of how these systems of divination manage to neither speak nor keep silent, but signify, and how the mind reacts to such symbols to build knowledge out of the seemingly random patterns of pieces of cardboard. There's nothing wrong with books listing card meanings and spreads, and those books certainly exist and are helpful and useful. And a traditional approach to the Lenormand would be just that: a list of meanings and combinations and how to read a few spreads. This book is a nontraditional approach exploring not just how to read the cards but how reading those cards changes our perception of knowledge and ultimately our lives.

The eighteenth century was the golden age of cartomancy: from it come two systems, the tarot and the Lenormand, and as we'll see in the early chapters of this book, each of these systems reflects one of the dominant philosophical schools of thought of the time. The tarot was reworked to reflect Neoclassical Neoplatonism, especially as it was understood in the Renaissance; the Lenormand was invented to reflect the new Romantic sensibility, honoring the power of nature and the individual. In later chapters, we will explore not only the theories of divination but the methods and procedures. We'll end with a discussion of the use of divination systems to create change in the world, to perform magic.

CHAPTER I

What Is the Lenormand?

Mademoiselle Marie-Anne Lenormand was a French fortune-teller who lived during the reign of Napoleon. With her card readings—and a wide range of other divinatory arts—she worked her way into the parties and gatherings of high society, and eventually into their money as well. She came to be known as the "Sibyl of the Salons," because she was a prophet like the ancient Roman sibyls who compiled their prophesies into the sibylline books. She died wealthy, despite her humble beginnings, but not before being imprisoned several times, either on charges of fortune-telling or, as she claims, because of the startling accuracy of her prediction of Napoleon's divorce.

She read her apparently dangerously accurate fortunes with various decks, mostly—it appears—playing cards, although on some of them she had drawn images and keywords. What we know of those images and keywords is limited to a sketchy eyewitness account. But when she died, several people came forward as her former apprentices, despite her insisting while she was alive that she never had taken a pupil.

The claim of being Mlle. Lenormand's apprentice no doubt gained a handful of card shufflers a free reputation, but we have to regard these claims with doubt. What we don't need to doubt is that Mlle. Lenormand cast a life-giving ray of light on the field of European cartomancy. Soon, many competing schools sprang up and spread from France to the rest of Europe, and beyond. Mlle. Lenormand gave birth to a new archetype.

Previously, the card reader was a shady character, often ethnically (and with a large dollop of racism) associated with the Gypsy or Roma people. In the nineteenth century, Charlotte Brontë describes such a traveling psychic, whom she even calls a sibyl, in *Jane Eyre* (although it turns out to be Mr. Rochester in disguise):

> The library looked tranquil enough as I entered it, and the Sibyl—if Sibyl she were—was seated snugly enough in an easy-chair at the chimney-corner. She had on a red cloak and a black bonnet: or rather, a broad- brimmed gipsy hat, tied down with a striped handkerchief under her chin. An extinguished candle stood on the table; she was bending over the fire, and seemed reading in a little black book, like a prayer-book, by the light of the blaze: she muttered the words to herself, as most old women do, while she read; she did not desist immediately on my entrance: it appeared she wished to finish a paragraph.
>
> I stood on the rug and warmed my hands, which were rather cold with sitting at a distance from the drawing-room fire. I felt now as composed as ever I did in my life: there was nothing indeed in the gipsy's appearance to trouble one's calm. She shut her book and slowly looked up; her hat-brim partially shaded her face, yet I could see, as she raised it, that it was a strange one. It looked all brown and black: elf-locks bristled out from beneath a white band which passed under her chin, and

came half over her cheeks, or rather jaws: her eye confronted me at once, with a bold and direct gaze.[2]

This passage describes a person of doubtful character and is meant to imply ethnic origins. It's actually a man in disguise, but Jane does not know this at this point. The other women at the party find themselves disturbed and excited by the "gipsy," but Jane, being a practical nineteenth-century woman, faces the stranger with equanimity born of a modern skepticism (although later, when the "gipsy" offers to read her head bumps, Jane regards this as a scientific method of fortune-telling).

Unlike this kind of traveling fortune-teller, who often as not found herself tossed out of the house from worries of theft and fraud, Mlle. Lenormand was a commanding yet thoroughly genteel presence. Captain R. H. Gronow describes her salon as being rather ordinary:

> I was first admitted into a good-sized drawing-room, plainly but comfortably furnished, with books and newspapers about, as one sees them at a dentist's. Two or three ladies were already there, who, from their quiet dress and the haste with which they drew down their veils, or got up and looked out of the window, evidently belonged to the upper ten thousand.[3]

Later, however, Gronow describes her reading chamber as "covered with huge bats, nailed by their wings to the ceiling, stuffed owls, cabalistic signs, skeletons—in short, everything that was likely to impress a weak or superstitious mind."[4]

Gronow also makes an effort to describe the cards themselves, but all he can say is that they are covered "with all kinds of strange

---

2. Charlotte Brontë, *Jane Eyre* (New York: Random House, 2000), 291.

3. R. H. Gronow, *Celebrities of London and Paris* (London: Smith, Elder & Co., 1865), 66.

4. Ibid., 67.

figures and ciphers depicted on them."[5] We also discover that she used two decks: the *grand* and the *petit jeu*. This, at least, is not much of a mystery: we know that cartomancers in the eighteenth century mostly used abbreviated decks. Rarely did they use a full deck of fifty-two cards. Other accounts describe her mixing cards from various kinds of decks, adding tarot cards to decks of what we would regard as playing cards, and so on.[6]

The meanings she gave each of the cards are lost; in her own writings, she rarely gives specific insight into how she reads the cards. A deck of thirty-six cards was published in 1845, after her death, each with an image supposedly attributed to a playing card by Mlle. Lenormand. This deck derived from a game, much as the tarot did. The original game—*Das Spiel der Hofnung* [sic]—also contained instructions for how to use the deck to tell fortunes. The images were only later repurposed solely to divination, and Mlle. Lenormand's name was affixed as a marketing strategy. This deck of thirty-six cards, now called the Petit Lenormand, quickly became popular due to its evocative yet everyday images.[7]

This deck became one of the most popular divination decks in Europe. I am told that even today, the Petit Lenormand is more commonly used for divination than the tarot in some places in Germany. While the tarot is the most popular divination deck in America, the Petit Lenormand is not completely unknown here. Yet resources on the Lenormand in the United States are few and far between, and vary in quality. We know, though, that this was not the deck that Mlle. Lenormand herself used, which does not erode its efficacy or its value.

Each region has its own method of reading the cards, so that one might speak of a French method, a German method, a South American method, and so on. An American method has yet to arise,

---

5. Ibid., 67

6. Ronald Decker, Thierry Depaulis, and Michael Dummett, *A Wicked Pack of Cards: The Origins of the Occult Tarot* (New York: St. Martin's Press, 1996), 138.

7. Ibid., 141.

however, although there are hints of a developing system, outlined in publications like Sylvie Steinbach's *The Secrets of the Lenormand Oracle*. Ms. Steinbach, a French immigrant who now makes her home in Los Angeles and her living by reading cards for the wealthy of the West Coast, describes a system she herself invented for the cards after years of reading. As one of the few books on the Lenormand in English, this text has had a large influence on the small community of American Lenormand readers.

This lack of resources is, in some ways, good news. After all, if one wishes to learn the tarot, one can plunge into infinite complexity immediately. Just earlier today, I browsed the tarot section at an occult bookstore. I could have filled my arms with books I had not read…although it would have emptied my pockets. But if I wish to dip my toe into the Lenormand, I must begin with the cards themselves.

And that's as it should be. The Lenormand speaks in plain language, and its symbols are the everyday archetypes of our lives. The two systems of symbols can be extremely productive together, not just for fortune-telling, but for divination, contemplation, creativity, and magic.

Fortunately, Lenormand decks are inexpensive. One can get several decks of Petit Lenormand for the price of a single tarot deck. And the images on the Lenormand are so simple that one can make an attractive deck oneself even with limited artistic talent. In a pinch, you can even make your own Lenormand out of a deck of playing cards. I will describe such a method in the next chapter so that you can begin to explore the Lenormand yourself.

I also assume that you have some knowledge of the tarot. In case you don't, I will include a basic description and meaning of the twenty-two major arcana cards. As I said, the tarot's depth is limitless. So if you wish to go more in-depth, I'd recommend picking up Rachel Pollack's *Seventy-Eight Degrees of Wisdom*, a classic text on the tarot. If you're already familiar with the tarot, it may be helpful to look over my description of the twenty-two major arcana, simply to see where I'm coming from.

To get the most out of this book, you'll need a deck of tarot cards and a deck of the Petit Jeu of Lenormand. For beginners, I recommend a tarot deck using the Rider-Waite imagery, such as the Lo Scarabeo Universal Tarot, used in this book. That covers a large number of decks indeed, so I'd suggest finding one that seems to appeal to you. However, extremely innovative decks (as if the Rider-Waite wasn't itself innovative!) might not work as well in terms of the symbolic synergy I'll discuss later. As for Lenormand decks, any of the thirty-six-card Petit Jeu will do. Selecting a deck is a matter of taste. The only warning I can offer in selecting a Lenormand deck is to avoid Gypsy Witch-style decks, which are related but not the subject of this book. Also avoid the Grand Jeu—a fifty-four-card fortune-telling deck. It's fine in its own regard as a divination deck, and is interesting itself, but not the subject of this book. If there are more or fewer than thirty-six cards, and the first card does not depict a man on horseback, you probably do not have the right kind of Lenormand deck for this book.

The Lo Scarabeo Petit Lenormand is attractive and popular, but unfortunately currently out of print. Do not mistake it for the Lo Scarabeo Lenormand Tarot, which is interesting but not a Petit Jeu. You can also find a deck like the Mystical Lenormand, painted by Urban Trösch, which has evocative and interesting images. Many people like the Piatnik deck with its soft images and playing card insets. The Lo Scarabeo French Cartomancy deck is also a suitable deck for beginners, and is the deck used in the illustrations in this book.

In general, Petit Lenormand decks come in three flavors. The first and simplest are simply images and, often, numbers. So the first card, the Rider, is just the number 1 and a picture of a man on a horse. The second, Clover, is a picture of a clover and the number 2, and so on. Some decks, like the Mystical Lenormand might include other symbols and images. The second kind of deck is the inset deck, which contains an inset or "medallion" of a playing card. The very popular Piatnik deck is one of these, as is the French Cartomancy deck. These are often good decks for beginners because court cards are sometimes regarded as representative not only of ideas but of people. So one might look at 4–House and notice that it has the King of Hearts. It might represent your house, then, but also your landlord, a person connected with houses. The third type of Lenormand contains an interpretive poem instead of a playing card inset. These can be found in English, but are particularly common in German. Such poems might help you remember meanings, but you'll find that the memory load with the Lenormand is much less than that required to read tarot effectively. I personally find such poems distracting, not to mention aesthetically unpleasant (at least, the ones in English tend not to be high literature). I usually use two decks, the Mystical for reading for others, and the Piatnik for reading for myself. The Mystical, for reasons having to do more with the sturdiness of the box than anything else, is also my traveling deck. Lenormand decks are inexpensive. Snap up what you can while you can; they go in and out of print unpredictably.

Another option is to make your own Lenormand out of playing cards. This is actually how I began with the Lenormand. If you have artistic skill, you can get blank cards and sketch your own cards. You can also use a regular deck of playing cards and write the titles on each card. You may also wish to create a small, simple drawing of the card's image. If you go this route, I find a Sharpie to work well on marking most cards. This option is economical if you are unsure you'll want to incorporate the Lenormand into your regular divination and contemplative practice and just want to try it out.

But after reading this book, and more importantly, after playing with the Petit Jeu, I know that you will find it as evocative as I have.

CHAPTER II

The Meanings of the Lenormand Cards and Making Your Own Deck

The Petit Jeu or Petit Lenormand consists of thirty-six cards numbered from one to thirty-six. These cards are traditionally associated with playing cards, although the sequence of the cards as numbered does not have any clear association with the suits or number of the playing cards.

Below I will describe the image on each card (which, unlike the tarot, is a simple task). I'll offer which playing card is associated with each card, so you can either make your own deck out of a deck of playing cards, or perhaps make a note of it on your homemade cards if you think it'll be useful knowledge later. I will also offer some "meaning starters."

I think it's a mistake to give the traditional sort of set meanings one sometimes sees in cartomancy manuals.[8] "Mistake" might be the wrong word there, but offering a set list of meanings limits the opportunities the Lenormand offers to mystics and magicians. We have this set of symbols and, at least in my case, scant French and no German. So we need to figure out what they mean to us before we start looking at what they mean elsewhere. I've found these symbols precise and flexible, at the same time. It's a strange paradox: these are both universal symbols and also personal ones.

So instead I will offer "meaning starters," suggested keywords and questions that you can modify as you go. At the same time, I'd be remiss not to mention, at least, some of the traditional meanings of these cards and how those meanings have shifted over time. Sylvie Steinbach, particularly, has changed several traditional meanings of the cards, and those controversial choices deserve some discussion.

I hope, however, that you'll make your own controversies eventually.

For each card, consider some or all of the following questions. You can do this in order, or you can just draw a new card every day and spend a few moments contemplating one of the questions. I find this activity always bears fruit, and at the very least will make long waits in lines somewhat more bearable. It's fun to try to think of which cards describe the people standing around me.

---

8. But of course some people will insist that I make that mistake, and so for them I've included a longer meditation on the meanings of each of the Lenormand cards in the appendix.

Meaning Starters

1. What everyday objects in your life does this card describe?

2. What kind of person does it describe? Do you have any friends or acquaintances that fit this card?

3. Think of a keyword—a noun or a verb or an adjective—that isn't listed below which helps you understand what the card means.

4. Write your own poetry for this card, three or four lines that describe how you imagine the card could work out in a reading.

5. What personal quality, virtue, or vice might this card refer to in your own personality?

6. If this card were a _____, what kind of _____ would it be? (If Lily were a car, would it be a classic car? If Tree described a trip, might it be a nature hike? Or a health spa?)[9]

---

9. These exercises are inspired by similar exercises in Juan García Ferrer, *El Método Lenormand: Todo Sobre las Cartas Lenormand* (Raleigh, NC: Lulu.com, 2008). I address this exercise more fully in chapter eleven.

The Lenormand Deck

1–Rider

A man on horseback travels down a road to his destination.

Keywords: Travel. Visitors/Visits. Go. Quick.

Playing Card: 9 of Hearts

2–Clover

A clover.

Keywords: Luck. Unexpected but pleasant. Serendipitous.

Playing Card: 6 of Diamonds

3–Ship

A ship at full sail sails across the ocean.

Keywords: Long distance travel. Far away. Foreign.

Playing Card: 10 of Spades

4–HOUSE
A small house or cottage.
Keywords: Home. Family.
Playing Card: King of Hearts

5–TREE
A thriving tree.
Keywords: Health. Spiritual. Body.
Playing Card: 7 of Hearts

6–CLOUDS
Clouds, dark on one side and light on the
other, nearly cover the sky.
Keywords: Confusion. Unclear.
Playing Card: King of Clubs

7–SNAKE
A coiled snake, ready to strike.
Keywords: Betrayal. Vice.
Devious. Deception.
Playing Card: Queen of Clubs

8–COFFIN
A coffin lies out for viewing.
Keywords: End. Change.
Playing Card: 9 of Diamonds

9–FLOWERS (SOMETIMES BOUQUET)
A bouquet of flowers,
cut and ready for the vase.
Keywords: Beautiful. Pleasant. Gift.
Playing Card: Queen of Spades

10–SCYTHE

*A scythe, lying with the blade
facing in one direction.*
Keywords: Cut. End. Choose.
Playing Card: Jack of Diamonds

11–WHIP (SOMETIMES BIRCH OR BROOM)

*A whip, birch rod, or broom,
hanging ready for use*
Keywords: Strenuous. Pain.
(According to Sylvie Steinbach, sex.)
Playing Card: Jack of Clubs

12–BIRDS (SOMETIMES OWLS)

*A collection of birds sitting on a
branch or wire; sometimes, two owls.*
Keywords: Talk. Speak.
Conversation. Rumor.
Playing Card: 7 of Diamonds

13–CHILD

A small, innocent child playing or running.
Keywords: Young. Small. Innocent. New.
Playing Card: Jack of Spades

14–FOX

A fox hiding or evading dogs, or foraging.
Keywords: Clever. Deceive. (According to Sylvie Steinbach, work and employment.)
Playing Card: 9 of Clubs

15–BEAR

A bear on its hind legs.
Keywords: Power. Strength. Boss. (According to Sylvie Steinbach, cash flow.)
Playing Card: 10 of Clubs

16–STARS

One or several stars in a clear night sky.

Keywords: Success. Vision. Occult. Mind.

Playing Card: 6 of Hearts

17–STORK

A stork sitting on the chimney of a house.

Keywords: Change. Improvement.

Playing Card: Queen of Hearts

18–DOG

A dog, sitting and waiting for its master.

Keywords: Friend. Familiar. Loyal.

Playing Card: 10 of Hearts

19–TOWER
A high tower or castle.
Keywords: Official. Institution.
Govern. Tall.
Playing Card: 6 of Spades

20–GARDEN (OR PARK)
A public garden, often with
a fountain and paths.
Keywords: Public. Gathering. People.
Playing Card: 8 of Spades

21–MOUNTAIN
A high and cold mountain.
Keywords: Obstacle. Wall. Delay.
Playing Card: 8 of Clubs

22–CROSSROADS
A path or road forks; a traveler
may stand at the fork.
Keywords: Options. Multiple. Progress.
Playing Card: Queen of Diamonds

23–MICE
A mouse or several mice eating some crumbs.
Keywords: Loss. Annoy. Waste.
Playing Card: 7 of Clubs

24–HEART
A Valentine-style heart.
Keywords: Love. Emotion. Happy.
Playing Card: Jack of Hearts

25–Ring

A wedding ring.

Keywords: Agreement. Marriage. Contract. Circle.

Playing Card: Ace of Spades

26–Book

A book open or closed, siting on a desk or lectern.

Keywords: Learning. Writing. Secret. Occult. Memory.

Playing Card: 10 of Diamonds

27–Letter

A sealed letter, waiting to be read.

Keywords: Written communication. Document. Certificate.

Playing Card: 7 of Spades

28–GENTLEMAN (OR MAN)
A man, in many decks pictured
reading a letter in a garden.
Keywords: The querent if male;
otherwise, a man.
Playing Card: Ace of Hearts

29–LADY (OR WOMAN)
A woman, often richly dressed.
Keywords: The querent if female;
otherwise, a woman.
Playing Card: Ace of Spades

30–LILY (OR LILIES)
A pure white lily.
Keywords: Complete. Peace. Old. Wise.
(In the German tradition, sex.)
Playing Card: King of Spades

31–SUN
A bright sun in a cloudless sky.
Keywords: Ego. Outward self. Heat.
Bright. Success.
Playing Card: Ace of Diamonds

32–MOON
A full or crescent moon.
Keywords: Inner self. Emotions.
Fame. Intuition. Dreams.
Playing Card: 8 of Hearts

33–KEY
An old-fashioned skeleton key.
Keywords: Aha! Fate. Pay attention! Yes.
Playing Card: 8 of Diamonds

34–FISH
Fish swimming in the sea.
Keywords: Independent.
Wealth. Freedom. Adventure.
Playing Card: King of Diamonds

35–ANCHOR
An anchor on the beach,
or sometimes below the waves.
Keywords: Stable. Lifestyle.
Persevere. Lasting.
Playing Card: 9 of Spades

36–CROSS
A cross, hanging from a chain or
planted as a monument to the dead.
Keywords: Burden. Worry. Pain.
Religion.
Playing Card: 6 of Clubs

We'll talk more about it later, but I should mention now that these thirty-six limited meanings can actually become infinitely complex through combination. For example, 25–Ring is a contract. What kind of contract? If it's followed by 26–Book, perhaps a publishing contract. Followed by 35–Anchor, an unbreakable one. Followed by 36–Cross? A religious oath. And 23–Mice: a disadvantageous one.

Now that you're armed with the basic meaning of these thirty-six cards, you can begin exploring your own deck, either one you buy or one you make. If you wish to make your own deck, either because you don't wish to spend the money or because you feel such a homemade deck will be more personally meaningful, the process is easy.

I'm going to assume that you lack, as I do, much in the way of artistic ability. But all we really need are the basic images. You could also opt simply to write the name of the card on the appropriate playing cards, and forgo the images entirely. In that case, the images would be in your head. If you go this route, I'd suggest you carefully visualize each image as you write the name on the card.

Once you finish or purchase your deck, familiarize yourself with it. There are lots of ways to doing so, some ritual and some fairly casual. If you are attracted to a ritual, I assume you can construct your own. But the Lenormand thrives on familiarity and casualness, so I would suggest keeping rituals simple and domestic: lighting a candle, saying a prayer, and then engaging with the cards.

One easy way to familiarize yourself with the deck is to just go through it a few times over a couple days, naming each card as you turn it over, and perhaps reciting the keywords to it.

You can also introduce yourself to the cards by drawing a single card every day. Leave the card face down, and when you come home or just before you go to bed, flip it over. How did that card manifest itself during your day? This is an efficient and interesting way to build up your knowledge of each card, and can also work with the tarot.

A fun game with the Lenormand is ruining TV shows you like to watch. Before the start of a show you enjoy watching but haven't yet seen, ask the Lenormand, "What will happen on this show tonight?" Then turn over three cards. As you watch, try to match those three cards to the developments on the TV show. It seems like a silly use of the cards, and I can't imagine many tarot readers doing such a thing with their oh-so-dignified decks, but the Lenormand is like a friend. And we do, after all, watch TV with our friends.

CHAPTER III

A Brief Description
of the Major Arcana

Since one of the purposes of this book is to explore the relationship between the tarot and the Petit Lenormand, it's necessary to establish what I mean by "tarot." Most readers—probably most people in general—have some notion what the tarot is, even if they're not sure how to pronounce it. But there are some misconceptions (some that I have even helped spread, unintentionally) so I'm going to quickly cover its history and then explain meanings of the twenty-two major arcana cards, at least as I see them. I imagine most of my readers will have their own meanings, and that's fine, but it's worth establishing a baseline.

The tarot is a fifteenth-century invention, so it pre-dates the Lenormand by centuries. However, we don't have much evidence of divination with the tarot until the eighteenth century. Therefore, the tarot and the Lenormand are closer siblings than might be supposed. Still, the images of the tarot are older: the tarot borrows from a medieval world long since passed by the time they were used for divination.

Prior to its use in divination, the tarot was used to play card games. These games, similar to Bridge, involve the taking of tricks, and as far as we can tell there was no esoteric meaning behind the games themselves. Moreover, there wasn't much standardization between decks. Early decks vary in the number of cards, especially in what we now call the major arcana and what were then called the trumps. The fixed order and images of the trumps are relatively late. And the purpose of the trumps, at least as far as early tarot goes, was to take tricks and thus score points.

We do have some religious proclamations against the tarot, not for any perceived magical characteristics of the decks, but because they were used in gambling. Sometimes, condemnations—usually in the form of outdoor sermons, such as those by San Bernardino di Siena, a fifteenth-century Franciscan—were followed by a "bon-fire of the vanities," what we now refer to as a book-burning. The items burned along with tarot and playing cards often included other games, such as backgammon sets and similar items, as well as "temp-tations" such as make-up and books of poetry.

Like many others, I used to think that playing cards derived from the tarot. It's a reasonable assumption. Unfortunately, it's wrong. We now know that playing cards probably pre-date the tarot. The earliest four-suit, fifty-two-card decks we have date from the late fourteenth century. Our earliest tarot decks, however, date from the early fif-teenth century. It's now generally thought that the tarot resulted from the adding of the trumps to a variant deck of playing cards.

At this time (the early fifteenth century) we have a situation where multiple card games have their own decks, and the purpose of those decks is gaming. Symbols of some important ideas appear in the trumps: virtues, vices, figures from mythology. But these began as decorations: the cards represent nothing, ultimately, but numbers to be used to determine the rank of trumps.

It's also common to hear that the Fool, the unnumbered trump in the early tarot decks, became the joker in modern playing decks; however, there's overwhelming evidence that the joker was intro-duced in America in the nineteenth century. A good story falls apart.

Over time, esoteric images began to appear on the cards. And that's really no mystery: when the tarot and playing cards both began to be used for divination, esoteric images were added to the more pictorial of the two. And in the early twentieth century, when A. E. Waite designed his tarot deck with the help of the artist Pamela Colman Smith, he (or, more likely, she) added pictorial elements to the minor arcana, or pip cards.

For our purposes, I want to focus mostly on the major arcana. The relationship between the images of the major arcana and those of the Lenormand is fruitful. I also wish to focus on the esoteric or inner meaning of these symbols; obviously the tarot was used to play games at one time (and, in Europe, still is). But both the tarot and the Lenormand have an almost equally long tradition of divination.

The major arcana of the tarot has twenty-two cards. I will discuss the images on the Rider-Waite-inspired Universal Tarot cards that follow, which will probably match most decks you select. However, an older deck has some popularity among tarot diviners: the Tarot de Marseilles, which differs in some regards from the Rider-Waite. I'll point out interesting variants as they occur, as well as some keywords for meaning. My descriptions are cursory; you'll find fuller descriptions and meditations on the tarot in Rachel Pollack's *Seventy-Eight Degrees of Wisdom*, a classic on the tarot.[10]

---

10. Rachel Pollack, *Seventy-Eight Degrees of Wisdom: A Book of Tarot* (San Francisco: Weiser, 1997).

The Tarot Trumps

0–THE FOOL

A young man chased by (or accompanied by) a dog is about to step off a cliff. He's holding a bundle.

Keywords: Beginning. Folly. Innocence.

I–THE MAGICIAN

A magician dressed in ceremonial robes stands before a table set with his elemental tools. He holds his arms in a posture indicating the union between above and below, an important occult maxim.

Keywords: Skill. Praxis.

II–THE HIGH PRIESTESS

A woman sits on a chair, a scroll in her hand. Behind her is the veiled entrance to the sanctum. In the Marseilles decks, she is the Papesse, a female pope.

Keywords: Wisdom. Theory. Secrets.

III–THE EMPRESS

A woman sits on her throne in a natural setting, a heart-shaped shield emblazoned with the sign of Venus at her feet.
Keywords: Love. Nature.

IV–THE EMPEROR

A man sits on his throne, a mountain behind him. He holds the tools of power.
Keywords: Authority. Civilization.

V–THE HIEROPHANT

A man sits on a throne, two acolytes kneeling before him. He holds his hands in a blessing gesture. In the Marseilles, this is the Pope.
Keywords: Education. Dogma. Convention.

VI–THE LOVERS

Two people stand with an angel blessing their union. A tree in the background hints that this is Eden. In the Marseilles, a man stands between two women and Cupid hovers above him.
Keywords: Choice. Union.

VII–THE CHARIOT

A man drives a chariot pulled by two sphinxes of different colors. In the Marseilles, these are horses.
Keywords: Progress. Will.

VIII–STRENGTH

A woman wrestles a lion. In the Marseilles, this is card XI.
Keywords: Strength. Power. Life.

IX–THE HERMIT

A lone man on a mountain
shines a light in the darkness.
Keywords: Seeking. Teaching.

X–THE WHEEL OF FORTUNE

A wheel inscribed with mystic signs
spins, while four mystical creatures
watch from the corners.
Keywords: Reversal of fortune. Luck.
Improvement.

XI–JUSTICE

A woman, blindfolded, holds aloft a
sword and scales. In the Marseilles,
this is card VIII.
Keywords: Balance. Redress.

XII–THE HANGED MAN

A man hangs upside down, his arms and legs folded into a mystical symbol.
Keywords: Sacrifice. Stasis. Initiation.

XIII–DEATH

A skeletal figure on a horse receives tribute from a bishop on a field filled with death. A child plays below. In the Marseilles, Death reaps the dead with a scythe. Often, in the Marseilles, this card is unnamed.
Keywords: Transformation. Endings.

XIV–TEMPERANCE

An angel, one foot on land and one in water, mixes water from one cup to another.
Keywords: Art. Care.

XV–THE DEVIL

The devil sits above two chained figures, offering them a sign of ironic blessing.
Keywords: Bondage. Matter.

XVI–THE TOWER

Two figures fall from a tower blasted by heaven. In the Marseilles, this card is called the House of God.
Keywords: Destruction. Violent transformation.

XVII–THE STAR

A woman, nude, pours water into a pond and onto the ground. A large star shines above her in a starry sky.
Keywords: Hope. Spiritual love.

XVIII–THE MOON

Two canines howl at a moon rising between two towers. A road weaves between the towers.

Keywords: Deception. Intuition. Mystery.

XIX–THE SUN

A child plays on a horse below a shining sun. In the Marseilles, two children play, with no horse.

Keywords: Joy. Success. Blessing.

XX–JUDGEMENT

The dead rise from coffins at the blast of an angel's trumpet.

Keywords: Advancement. New phase of life.

XXI–THE WORLD

*A hermaphrodite dances in a wreath while
the four mystical animals look on.*
Keywords: Completion. Perfection.

These thumbnail sketches illustrate the domain of the major arcana. These are major concerns, almost philosophical in nature. When compared to the Lenormand, the Lenormand seems almost trivial. But is it? When we compare these symbols, we'll discover an interesting disjunction between fortune-telling and divination, and as we'll see, the roots of that disjunction not in esoteric purity but in social class.

CHAPTER IV

Occult Symbolism and the Anima Mundi

Here I am driving in the western suburbs of Chicago. I'm singing along to The Killers on the radio and trying not to think about the fact that I just absentmindedly took a swig from the three-day-old cup of coffee in my cup holder. My mind is, to say the least, occupied, but I nevertheless press on the brake pedal when I see the octagonal sign ordering me to STOP. It doesn't matter whether or not the words are there; I don't read the sign as a word. I read it as a symbol that leads to a physical reaction before it ever meets my conscious mind.

I do more than stop, though. Because of that sign, I know that I have to analyze the situation in certain ways. First, I have to realize how many signs there are. If there are only two, then I have to show some care to cross-traffic. But no, there are four. So I have to recognize which cars have right of way. I time which of us gets to the sign first, but two of us come to the sign at the same moment. The white Ford to my right and I have a photo-finish race to the sign, so I glance at the driver and nod, and he pulls forward cautiously. As soon as he's through the intersection, I start rolling cautiously, making eye-contact with the other drivers.

I do all this during about three bars of the chorus of "Human." Now, I'm a clever guy, but the guy in the Ford kind of looked like he would have a hard time tying his shoes without a diagram, and I know for a fact that some of the people on the streets can't do simple math in their head or read without moving their lips. Plus, I'm such a genius that I forgot to throw out the old unfinished coffee in my cup holder—and worse, I drink it without thinking days later. How is it possible that nearly all of them—and me, on a very bad day—can interpret such a complex symbolic system so easily?

All humans are geniuses at one thing: interpreting symbols. No matter their level of intelligence, they're capable of using language unless they're suffering a specific form of brain damage. One may not know as many words as another, just as some may not know Hungarian, but they can express any thought they have and understand any idea couched in words they know. Language is nothing less than a complicated symbol system, much more complicated than mere traffic signs.

The old definition of symbol is "anything that stands in place of something else." A stop sign stands in place of the act of the stopping. The word "orchid" stands in place of the green thing not getting enough sunlight in my living room. This definition is fine as far as it goes, but it doesn't take into account that symbols don't actually exist in isolation. A stop sign means very little hanging on a dormitory wall. It has to exist in the system of other traffic signs. If I hung up a piece of paper with the word "stop" typed on it, it would have no effect whatsoever other than to confuse people. It's still a symbol standing in place of the act of stopping, but it doesn't work because it's not part of the system.

That system exists only in the minds of the people who use it. A symbol has no independent existence outside of the mind. Note, however, that "people" is plural. If I walk around speaking a made-up language, I cannot be said to be communicating unless someone else learns it. It's not that the language is made-up that makes it unreal—

after all, I can speak to someone in Esperanto or, if I take the time to learn it, Klingon, and be understood—but that it is not part of a shared system.

This shared system does not exist only in human minds, however. Or at least, so I would contend as a panpsychist. A panpsychist believes there is a mind underlying all of reality. I could call it "God" perhaps, but it's not much like the traditional God of Islam or Judeo-Christianity. Instead, I'll call it by the name the ancients gave it: the Anima Mundi, or "soul of the universe." The Anima Mundi is a mind as well, and it shares some symbols with us. It probably doesn't pay much attention to traffic signs, but like all of us, it's interested in the symbols that refer to parts of itself. If we want to get someone's attention at a party, we start talking about their lives. Similarly, if we want to get the attention of the Anima Mundi, we start using the symbols that refer to parts of it.

Those symbols themselves have a grammar, just as words in a language do or traffic signs do. The ancients, being clever little buggers, organized these symbols according to a general scheme of reality. This scheme, to the literal-minded, seems to suggest that the Earth is the center of the universe. In reality, however, the ancients recognized that, in the infinite, any perspective is the center. Therefore, just as maps made in America tend to put North America at the center of the world, they recognized that putting the Earth at the center made sense, since we happen to live there.

The image following, the Mirror of Nature, is a famous picture of the Anima Mundi made by Robert Fludd, and it served a specific purpose. Namely, it provided a thumbnail outline of the grammar of the symbols the Anima Mundi seemed to speak in, in a handy cheat-sheet like those laminated summaries of topics you can get at bookstores. It was a study and memory aid. Unfortunately, we've lost the art of organizing information in graphical form.

It is tempting to go into the meaning of every squiggle and symbol on this chart, but I heroically refrain, and instead will point out only two things. First, notice that the artistic style of this engraving shares some similarity with the art of the tarot, especially as it evolved into the nineteenth and twentieth centuries. It is clear that Waite and Smith were influenced by the symbolic grammar of this kind of diagram. Second, the woman at the top with the celestial pasties is the Anima Mundi, the soul of the world. To the Renaissance magician, she is the explanation for why divination works.

In the Neoplatonic worldview of the Renaissance magician, reality as we perceive it is a shadow of a living mind, the cosmic *nous* or consciousness. Everything that exists is a reflection of an idea or form in that Nous. The thing that governs the way those ideas work out in time and space is the psyche, or in Latin, the *anima*, usually translated "soul." The anima governs the processes of things. If the form is like a recipe for cookies, the anima is the process of gathering together all the ingredients and following that recipe to create material cookies. Our own soul is what governs the process of being a person, of being alive. The *mundus*, which means both "world" and "universe" in Latin, also has an anima or soul. It is the anima that gives a thing the power to act. The universe is alive, and it is conscious, and through divination we speak to it by giving it a place where it can act. This old philosophy is the root of a contemporary philosophy, panpsychism, which argues that all of reality is consciousness—not a mind in anyone's particular head, but Mind in general.

The materialist perspective is that the mind just grows out of matter: it arises as a side-effect of a particular chance arrangement of molecules, and any sense of self or feeling of free will is an illusion. Some studies have shown that, for example, the neurons in our brain begin the process of carrying out a choice before we are conscious of making the choice. If you decide to move your arm above your head, your brain begins the process of starting the movement well before you decide that you desire to move your arm. One interpretation of this data is that our choices are illusory; another interpretation is that our choices are not illusions, but we are not always self-aware of every bit of our consciousness. If consciousness resides, even in some rudimentary form, in the cells of our brain—or, for that matter, the very molecules of our flesh—then it might stand to reason that such a consciousness could affect the body itself without our self-awareness figuring into it.

One panpsychist perspective is that matter instead grows out of mind. Consciousness, then, comes first, and matter is merely the grossest form of that consciousness, information given solidity and structure. DNA does not encode genetic information: DNA is genetic information made solid. When a piece of DNA unzips in order to replicate, that information isn't gone—it's still present, even if the DNA itself has changed form temporarily.

All this philosophy boils down to one point: if the universe is conscious, we can communicate with it. It is not, however, conscious the way you and I are conscious. It doesn't worry about its property taxes, make an appointment to have its piano tuned, or wonder if it should make another pot of coffee to get through the day's quota of writing. It does other stuff that we don't much worry about: calculating, over and over, various universal constants; giving rise to the structure of space and the directional arrow of time; ensuring and sustaining physical laws that allow matter to exist. So if I want to know which of the three piano tuners I'm considering to call, how could I get that information from the Anima Mundi?

First, we can't assume that English (or Polish or Russian or Spanish) is the language the Anima Mundi will speak. Clearly it's Latin, according to Fludd—and Latin written in a hinky handwriting … wait. No, actually, Fludd *does* give us the language the Anima Mundi speaks, very clearly in this diagram. The Anima Mundi speaks in symbols.

Now, how can we expect the Anima Mundi is capable of suggesting a piano technician? We can't specifically, but we do know that piano technicians are part of this universe, and share in the thoughts of the Anima Mundi. It's not as if the Anima Mundi thinks, "I've got to make sure that the strong nuclear force adheres these atoms together in these planets, but those piano tuners can take care of themselves—if they explode into a fine red mist, I don't care. I've got bigger stuff to worry about." It fortunately doesn't work that way (and good thing, too—my piano sits on a very nice rug).

So, how do we ask the Anima Mundi to recommend a piano technician? We home in on the issue—called the *quesited* in traditional astrology and geomancy—and we seek a pattern of symbols around it. We can do this by looking for omens—the flights of birds, the movement of clouds or lightning, whether or not various coincidences happen—but this method requires a level of intuition and self-honesty that isn't always easy to come by. Instead, we can address a particular pattern of symbols created through observation of the world, either in preexisting patterns (such as astrology) or in "randomly" created patterns (such as cartomancy).

Every culture has its own set of symbols just as every culture has its own languages. In many ways, the system of symbols used by a culture are a language, but one that's used specifically to talk to the Anima Mundi and understand her responses back. In the Western occult tradition, most systems of divination can be broken down into symbols in sets of two, three, four, seven, and twelve. Fludd's diagram gives us the symbols in sets of two, three, four, and seven, and also shows how they interact with matter.

Symbolic elements arranged in pairs naturally fall into the particular relationship of opposition. Similarly, symbols arranged in threes, fours, or sevens have a tendency to fall into similar patterns. Therefore, I refer to symbol systems by the number of items in them, which I will call their "key," as in a piece of music. Just as the key of music determines what relationships the notes will have with each other, the key of a symbol system determines the kinds of relationships the symbols will have. In the key of two, for example, we can have items that are opposites (like on and off, good and evil) or complements (like right and left) or the poles of a scale (like hot and cold). Any set of symbols based on the key of two will be arranged in one or several of these relationships.

In the key of two, we have the alchemical arts of *solve* and *coagula*, or separation and combination. These are the *no* and *yes* of the Anima Mundi, and the simplest oracle is, perhaps, the coin. Even complex systems of divination, such as astrology, can be reduced to a "yes" or a "no" answer.

When applied to cartomancy, we can see how symbols in both the tarot and the Lenormand are sometimes arranged according to the key of two. For example, we have 28–Gentlemen and 29–Lady, which exist in binary pairs; we also have 31–Sun and 32–Moon. We can see that objects in the key of two often come in sequence in the Lenormand. In the tarot, we have similar pairs: I–The Magician and II–The High Priestess and III–The Empress and IV–The Emperor, among others. Again, we see these binary pairs often represented in sequential cards. In addition, there are some cards that contain the idea of twoness in themselves, such as VI–The Lovers in the tarot and 22–Crossroad or 12–Birds in the Lenormand. But you can only go so far with the key of two. Not every question can be reduced to a yes or a no, and playing Twenty Questions with the Anima Mundi isn't efficient.

More complex scales of symbols are therefore necessary. Each of the more complex scales begins with the scale of two, however. Reality probably isn't dualistic, but our minds are and we experience the world as if it is organized in pairs. Deconstructionist philosophers have shown that the duality we take for granted is arbitrary, and so is language. "Arbitrary" doesn't mean "not useful" or even "unreal." It merely means it has no *necessary* connection to reality. But since the nature of "reality" itself is a vexed question to the appropriately skeptical magician, there's no real reason to expect our symbols systems to be identical to the territory they map.

If we add a middle element to the scale of two, we have the scale of three. In Fludd, this scale manifests as the three kingdoms of mineral, plant, and animal. In astrology, they appear as the three qualities of fixed, cardinal, and mutable. And in alchemy, they appear as salt, mercury, and sulfur. I'll refer to them by their astrological names, only because it'll become important when we get to the scale of twelve later. The fixed quality is the essence of stability and form. But nothing remains unchanging. The force that causes the change of form is the cardinal (from the Latin word for "hinge") quality, represented in alchemy by mercury, which hovers between liquid and solid. The instability that results is the quality of mutable.

If you take two different forms of the key of two, and place them across each other as in the figure on the facing page, you'll see they create a key of four. For the four elements, these two polar opposites are hot and cold; dry and moist. Air is hot and moist. Fire is hot and dry. Water is cold and moist. Earth is cold and dry. Of course, nothing is completely dry or completely hot, which means any given thing falls between these two things in relationship to other things on the scale. A towel might be dry or moist, but only in relationship to other items. If it is drier than your skin, it'll feel dry. If it's moister than your skin, it'll feel moist. My coffee is warm, but only in relationship to ice-water, because it's been sitting there for a couple hours. And when someone spits out cold coffee, it's often the temperature that they'd spit out as "warm" in a soda. So a particular item isn't "earth" or "air." Instead, it's on a scale between four poles. The elements aren't four little boxes to put ideas in; they're more like four compass points to help us orient an object.

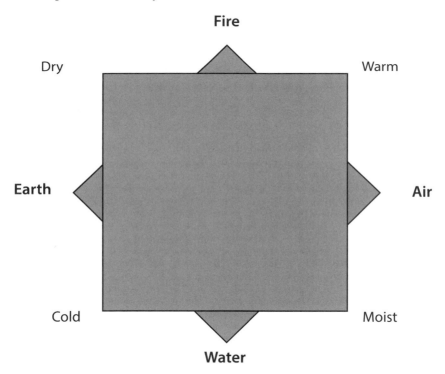

A lot of magicians don't know where this four-element system comes from, but the history is interesting and illuminating. Empedocles was a Sicilian philosopher born in about 490 BCE. As a Pre-Socratic, he was mostly concerned with questions of ontology or being. The main philosophical question of that time was about the basic stuff of reality. Different philosophers had different notions, but it was Empedocles who eventually came up with the notion that perhaps there were four different "roots" to reality, and that the complex relationships we observe are merely the interactions of these elements in combination.

It's easy to laugh at this theory as naive, but doing so would be an arrogant dismissal of what was really a sophisticated idea. Empedocles wasn't interested in figuring out atomic elements in the sense we use them now. He wanted to explain his observation of an ever-changing world, and in this he succeeded. He provided a heuristic that even those familiar with our more complex system of physical elements still adopt to explain phenomena.

Empedocles wanted to explain the physical universe, and in the action of matter he recognized two forces—love and strife—that contended against each other constantly, neither entirely winning and neither entirely devoid of the other. These forces were not just metaphoric: elements came together out of the same sort of love that humans felt for each other, and separated due to the same sort of strife. The elements were characters in a cosmic drama, or perhaps ideas arranged by successive acts of synthesis and analysis in the mind of the universe.

Many contemporary magicians use the elements as metaphors of emotional or mental states, and the understanding of Empedocles's panpsychism opens the door to this understanding. Perhaps it's not even metaphoric to say that a lake is calm—perhaps water and emotional states are linked underneath the surface of matter. Traditional and not-so-traditional correspondences abound. The advantage of making these correspondences is that it places our experiences into a framework. Just as the key of two offers a set number of relationships for the items placed in it, so the key of four creates a frame that describes relationships.

For example, fire and water are antithetical and cannot long endure each other. Similarly, we might say that the passions of lust and rage cannot long endure the emotional depth of water. That implies that these two elements are always in a condition of strife, which would lead to the entire universe arranging itself in a scale of two against water and fire. Since that has not happened, there must also be a way for love to bring the two together—and we can witness the judicious application of fire to water to create and transform and nourish: making soup, for example. And in human relationships, passion and strife do not lead to deep and meaningful relationships, while passion and love do.

The elements are not merely physical things, but exist in all worlds. Agrippa writes:

> The elements therefore are to be found everywhere, and in all things after their manner, no man can deny. First in these inferior bodies feculent, and gross, and in celestials more pure, and clear; but in supercelestials living, and in all respects blessed. Elements therefore in the exemplary world are Ideas of things to be produced, in intelligences are distributed powers, in heavens are virtues, and in inferior bodies gross forms.[11]

Therefore, if we can observe the interaction of elements in one world, we can assume the same interaction holds for other worlds as well.

Each of the four elements is associated with ideas in the mind of the Anima Mundi by metaphor. The element of earth is the idea of all solid things, both literally and metaphorically. Stability and materiality are the characteristics of earth. Earth is cold and therefore passive. In the world of human events, earth represents physical economy and the body. The idea of water is also passive, but unlike earth, changes according to its environment. In the world of human events, water—because it so easily combines together—represents relationships and the emotions that arise from them, both good and bad. Air, on the other hand, is active and pervasive, and so among human concerns represents thoughts and communication. At the same time, we know that air can be a destructive force, just as the mind can be, and therefore it also can represent strife, particularly strife arising from thoughts. Fire, unlike water, does not change according to circumstances, but causes

---

11. Henry Cornelius Agrippa, *Three Books of Occult Philosophy*, Donald Tyson. (Woodbury, MN: Llewellyn, 2007), 27.

change. It is also active and can represent those emotions we imagine to be "hot," as well as activity itself; therefore, it often symbolizes work and labor in human events.

The advantage of a symbol system like this is that it can reveal some relationships and exclude others. It organizes and categorizes thought, which allows communication. In other words, it provides a grammar of symbols we can use in divination to understand relationships between ideas we place within it. And we can classify certain cards in both decks by the element they seem to partake of (which may not be the element they are traditionally linked with in some systems). In the Lenormand, 21–Mountain is clearly earthy, while in the tarot, XI–Justice is very airy. And, of course, some cards again contain the whole key, such as XXI–The World in the tarot. Still, reducing everything to four categories may not be sufficient. And for Fludd and his contemporaries, the four elements were sublunary, meaning that they lay underneath the orbit of the moon. They were, therefore, best suited as symbolic placeholders for material, everyday things.

The key of seven, on the other hand, represented celestial ideas. In practice, plenty of emotional and intellectual ideas occur among the elements, and plenty of practical quotidian things occur in the symbol system of the seven planets. But in general, Renaissance and medieval magicians wanted to separate the functional world from the mental world. An easier way to conceive of the difference is in terms of change. The elements are in a constant change of flux, but the seven visible planets move slower and, with the exception of the moon and Mercury, represent ideas that work out longer in time and are more resistant to change.

The seven planets of antiquity, as well, influence both the physical world and the celestial world. It's possible to file everything in the world under some combination of elements and planets. According to the doctrine of signatures, everything reveals its inner nature by its outward appearance. So if you pick up a rock and look at it with full attention, and are familiar with the correspondences of the planets and elements, you'll soon see what pattern that rock holds in the mind of the Anima Mundi. Obviously, being a rock, it is of earth, but perhaps it is lighter than expected, which might indicate some air, and perhaps it is red, which might indicate fire and, in the planetary realm, Mars.

Just as the elements are not merely physical things, so the planets do not refer only to the celestial bodies. It would be safer to say that for the magician, the physical bodies of the planets are merely one manifestation of their power. Even if we had a different solar system, our experiences would still fall into these seven realms. We'd just not be able to use astrology to discuss them.

The moon isn't a planet according to scientific classifications, but those classifications are arbitrary, as those of us who still have Pluto in our memory can attest (I'm mostly annoyed that they ruined my perfectly good mnemonic for the planets: My very educated mother just served us nine pizzas. Now what is she going to serve us? Noodles?). For astrologers and magicians, a planet is merely a thing visible from Earth that moves across the sky in the ecliptic, the plain cut across the sphere of the heavens by the movement of the sun and moon. The moon, being the fastest of these moving objects and also the most changeable, is therefore the icon of change and speed. It's also large in the sky, roughly the size of the solar disk, and therefore represents the complement of the sun. It is visible both during the day and at night, but is the most impressive at night, and therefore represents those activities done at night: sleeping, dreaming, and sex.

Mercury isn't as fast or changeable as the moon, but it does have its phases and, because it orbits the sun faster than the Earth, we often observe it seeming to go backwards as it laps us. Other planets do this as well, but Mercury does it frequently, and therefore the ancients named this planet after the god who in Roman mythology acted as messenger of the gods. Mercury was also the gods of merchants, so that metaphoric association comes along with it as well, but overall Mercury represents the human activities of communication and thought. Mercury also represents technology, especially communication and travel technologies. Some people claim to experience more breakdowns in these types of devices during times of Mercury's retrograde (or backwards) motion, but I'm not sure if this is true or not. It may be a case of confirmation bias.

Venus is bright and has a milky white color when seen away from city lights. Like the other inner planets, it closely attends the sun, rising just before it or setting just after, and therefore it has been known as both the morning star and the evening star. The Greek name for the planet, Phosphorus, was later given to a flammable metal because it means "light bearer." The Latin calque of this word, *lucifer*, was used to describe both Christ and Satan, at different times. The Romans, however, identified this planet as Venus, their goddess of love, because of its brightness and beauty. For this reason, Venus rules over love, pleasure, sex, and beauty.

Mars, on the other hand, is named after the Roman god of war, or at least so everyone says. But Mars or Mavors was more than just the god of war to the Romans: he was the god of agriculture, civilization, honor, duty, and war. In other words, he was (well, is) the god of labor of all types, whether violent or not. Similarly, the planet does not just rule violence and discord, but also energy and force. The red color of Mars is caused by iron in the soil of the planet, an occasion where occultists hit it right before scientists did, as iron is the mineral ruled by Mars.

Sol, or the sun, was central to astrologers even before we developed the model of a heliocentric universe. The sun represents health, identity, ego, selfhood, honors, and creativity. How much of these associations are modern is difficult to determine. The ancient Romans and Greeks didn't have the same concept of ego that we have, nor would they regard selfhood as an unmitigated good as many Americans might. In Vedic astrology or Jyotish, the sun is not benevolent, as it can destroy the power of any planet near it, as well as indicate areas of potential problems if badly aspected. We sometimes forget that Apollo, the beautiful healer of ancient Greek mythology, was also the bringer of plague.

Jupiter, named after the Roman god Iuppiter, is a slow-moving and distant planet, which was early associated with the power and justice of its namesake god. In another interesting parallel of astrology and astronomy, astronomers later discovered that the physical Jupiter is extremely large and its considerable gravity well has captured an abundance of moons (sixty-seven, by last count). In that respect, it is indeed a lordly planet. In astrology, it represents power, justice, benevolence, and wealth.

Saturn, named after the Roman agricultural god Saturnus, governs systems and restrictions. Where Jupiter expands outward, Saturn pulls inward. For this reason, Saturn is sometimes regarded as a figure of malice in astrology, but just like the violent energy of Mars, the restrictions of Saturn placed in their appropriate place can be beneficial. Saturn is sometimes marked with the keywords of "contraction" or "restriction," but you can also think of it as crystallization or organization. Saturn is the planet of patterns and procedures, rules and laws, both in the sense of human laws and laws of nature.

As an aside, when I flip open an occult book asking myself if I want to buy it, I hate seeing a long list of definitions of things I already know. I know that some of my readers may be new to this symbolism, and some are now going, "Aw, darn it, astrology? Please." And others are making impatient "hurry up" motions in their minds. I sympathize, but the above list isn't just an introduction to the idea of each of the symbols: it illustrates my larger point, which is that all of human experience can be divided up into these categories, and we already do so whether we are familiar with astrological symbolism or not.

Here are four experiences: falling in love, seeing a beautiful painting, getting arrested, buying a new car. If we try to look at these experiences as material events, trying as best we can to eschew symbolism, we can see that they are all unrelated. But if you were to ask people which two are the most alike, most people would probably place falling in love and seeing a beautiful painting closer together than getting arrested or buying a car. You might get the occasional poet who regards love as a kind of prison, or the car aficionado who thinks getting a new car is a lot like love. But overall, most people regard love and beauty as related experiences. They already, without necessarily knowing the terms, lump them under Venus.

But if we're trying to come up with a set of symbols that can communicate human experience, we still need to account for that car collector or that cynical poet. How do we do that? We recognize that the domains of the planets interact and overlap. For example, you can mix the influences of Saturn and Venus in such as a way as to create a sense of love as imprisonment. You can also add the influence of Jupiter (and perhaps Mercury) to Venus to create a love for automobiles. In astrology, there are multiple ways such influence can derive, but this isn't a book on astrology so I will not go into extreme detail, as much as I might like to.

Instead, I want to once again call your attention to the Fludd drawing of the Mirror of Nature. The concentric rings in the center represent the orbits of the planets. You can see that these concentric rings spread out from a center point, and that several of the planets have lines connecting them to items in lower concentric rings. Renaissance magicians saw each planet not only potentially interacting with each other, but with the elements as well. It's common to speak of the planets sending out "rays," but one should be careful not to assume this description is necessarily physical. Although I'm sure some Renaissance magicians believed that literal rays emanated from the actual physical body of Mars, others recognized, I think, that the physical body of Mars is just the manifestation of the ray of something else—an Ideal Mars, if you will.

While we're on Mars, let's imagine that Mars sends a ray down through the concentric rings. In the world of matter, it manifests through the elements. In alchemy, we'd recognize Mars in Earth as iron, and Mars in water as Oil of Vitriol (what we now call sulfuric acid). We'd also recognize that Mars arises in the mental analogues of those elements. Mars in earth is the physical energy of the body; Mars in air is the strife of the mind; Mars in water is anger, and so on. It's not always immediately obvious which thing a given planet manifests as in a given element. Yet it's valuable to meditate on the possible permutations, both to familiarize yourself with the symbols and to begin to understand experience from a magical perspective. Keep in mind that *meaning is the interaction of symbols in a mind.*

The entire process is complicated by the fact that multiple rays may affect mixtures of elements. At this point, an attempt to tabulate the possible permutations becomes tempting but impossible. One would end up with a thesaurus of every possible experience, a work of endless labor and dubious value. However, if someone created such a thesaurus with detached pages, in such a way as they could arrange the basic combinations in endless other combinations, the labor might be reduced considerably. Moreover, such a book could be "read" by interpreting the relationships on the fly, instead of imagining ahead of time every single possible combination.

Most systems of divination are just that. They have tokens—in our case here, cards—that represent particular arrangements of elements. In astrology, for example, the seven planets move through twelve houses and twelve signs, each of which is composed of the key of four permuted through the key of three—so that, for example, you have fixed fire (Leo), mutable fire (Sagittarius), and so on.

Once you start looking, you begin to see these symbolic patterns everywhere—and this means that nearly anything can become a medium for communication with the Anima Mundi. When the magicians of the eighteenth-century occult revival stumbled across a popular card game that involved evocatively decorated cards, they immediately noticed patterns of symbolism that hinted to them that this system was something more than a card game. They began to modify the cards. Eliphas Levi went so far as to perform a wholesale editing of the symbolism, creating just such a thesaurus as mentioned earlier. Later decks, such as the Rider-Waite and the Crowley Thoth Tarot carried this process even further.

Was the tarot really a secret occult book hidden in the form of an innocuous card game? Maybe, although I am skeptical. It doesn't matter—even if humans intended only to make a fun game to pass a few hours, the Anima Mundi is always whispering to us in our unconscious, and so we may very well have created the cards, all unknowingly, to reflect her subtle language of symbols. In the next chapter, we'll explore how this cosmology or understanding of the universe can help us use cards to understand the mind of the world.

CHAPTER V

The Symbolic Structure of the Major Arcana (or, Throw Away Your Little White Book)

Buying a tarot card deck is not a complex procedure, even if you don't really know that much about tarot. Go to the bookstore. Look through the decks you like (there will be samples). Consider buying the Tarot of the Cat Lovers or the Tarot of the Autobots or something. Commune with your inner cat or inner robot. Look at the Dalí deck and imagine how impressed your friends will be. Find a deck that resonates with your inner being, then put it back and buy the Rider-Waite deck.

I'm only half-kidding. There's a bookshelf in my office stacked with various decks, all of which I've used and enjoyed. But when it comes to actually doing divination and magical work, I come back again and again to two decks: the Rider-Waite and the Crowley Thoth deck. And I would hate to pooh-pooh the artistic work of fellow occultists, but at least some (by which I mean, many) decks you find on display for sale are really rather awful. Many decks are gorgeous pieces of art and could work for divination—after all, you can find the language of the Anima

Mundi nearly everywhere. But there's something to be said for the tried and true.

Buy the deck you like. You will anyway, but let me make my case. Most decks are just knockoffs of the Rider-Waite deck anyway. To test, pick up a copy of both the Rider-Waite and some other deck (the Tarot of the Frat People, let's say). Now flip past the changes they make to the major arcana (replacing the Hierophant, perhaps, with the Pledgemaster). After all, Waite made a few such changes himself. Get to the minor arcana, the cards that represent the suits of tarot—wands, cups, swords, and disks (or pentacles). Odds are good that the Tarot of the Frat People will rename one or more of these suits, for no clear reason—paddles instead of wands, kegs instead of cups. Is there a clear symbolic reason why such a change seemed necessary? The tarot is supposed to describe every situation possible; why would changing one of the suits, or all of them, make it clearer symbolically what is going on in a life? Is there a reason that kegs represent the element of water better than cups? Also notice if the cards simply represent a number of the relevant objects: is the three of kegs just three kegs? The odds are against it: probably you'll see three people celebrating with three kegs, or something of that nature. It will probably look strikingly familiar to the Waite deck, because Waite (or Smith) invented these images in order to make the minor arcana easier to learn. Everyone else copied them, because they were such a good idea. And some of the copies might be better, in some senses, than the original. Many people, for example, prefer the redrawn Universal Tarot images depicted in this book.

The problem with making willy-nilly changes, though, is that the Rider-Waite deck is carefully designed to reflect the symbolism of both elemental and planetary interactions. The claim that Waite added blinds to the cards is probably true—after all, there's really no clear symbolic reason why the Six of Swords should have a boat, other than some traditional meanings of the cards. But how much worse is the unthinking copying of those blinds coupled with an unawareness of the actual symbolic parts?

I don't mean to imply that the Rider-Waite deck is the best of all available decks (I actually prefer the Crowley Thoth deck for having more careful symbolism), nor do I mean to imply that you should only like certain kinds of things. If you're into fraternities and you want to buy the Tarot of the Frat People, go ahead—but keep in mind that the tarot is both art and a tool. Maybe a glass hammer is really pretty, but it's not terribly practical.

Once you buy a deck, you'll find it comes with a little white book (LWB). This booklet supposedly tells you how to read the cards. It does little in the way of that, actually, but it might be useful in giving you a short bio of the artist, which is always interesting. When people buy their first tarot deck—and I remember doing this as a kid—they flip through the booklet frantically while doing readings, trying to piece together the somewhat vague "meanings" of the cards to their question. I must have had some success, since I didn't give up—but I do remember putting my tarot cards on a shelf for a couple years after buying them, because I couldn't figure out how the odd statements in the little book had anything to do with either the pictures on the cards or my question.

It's a daunting prospect as it's presented by that LWB. Seventy-eight cards, each with two meanings—most LWBs use reversed meanings even if the authors of the deck didn't. That seems like a lot of memorization before you can ever lay out a card, so most people don't bother and apologetically "use the book," flipping through the LWB as they read the cards. Even professional readers, when they read for themselves, often "use the book," although they rarely admit it.

As an aside, this holds true for astrology, too. You buy a book on astrology, cast your chart, and then look up what Mercury in Gemini means. You read a short paragraph, try to make sense of it, and then move on to the next planet-house combination. These instruction books, whether LWBs or cookbook astrology texts, rarely teach the synthesis of the information. In other words, the symbols are saying something—not a lot of little paragraphs of something.

Each card is an interaction of symbols with a particular meaning—not a bunch of unrelated meanings. And even though you could write a paragraph on any given card, given some intuition and thought, most readings don't work that way. If you learn the definitions of the cards from the LWB, you will learn them in a state of mind you do not use while you're doing a reading. Studies on state-dependent learning have shown conclusively that we recall best in the state of mind we learned the information. Mostly, scholars use this information to make jokes about taking tests while drunk, but it is relevant in divination. If we do not learn the meanings of the cards in the state of mind we intend to recall them—the divinatory state of consciousness—we will find it harder to read. Memorizing a book or, more likely, flipping through the thing while you read will not be conducive to this state of mind.

So here's the good news: you don't have to memorize seventy-eight paragraphs about the cards. You need only understand how their symbols interact. Similarly, in astrology, once you know how symbols interact, you don't really need thick interpretive tomes unless you want them. Even the LWB can be useful, and once you understand the symbols, you can gain hours of pleasant meditation thinking about how or why Waite thought the card meant "that." In fact, when I read for myself, I often "use the book" because I want to see what things I might know about the card but not be thinking about when I read for myself.

The first thing you need to do is learn the major arcana. The advantage of doing this is that you've got a divination deck you can use even before you've got the entire minor arcana learned, as the major arcana can stand alone.

You've got twenty-two cards to learn, and we're going to learn them in groups. If, as is likely, you've already memorized the twenty-two major trumps (or, for that matter, the seventy-eight cards of the deck), I hope that you'll bear with this exercise and perhaps even complete it, as a way to increase your understanding. Such a contemplation of the tarot seems like a beginner's exercise, but it's like a musician playing scales—there's no point at which musicians stop playing scales, and there's no point at which you graduate away from thinking about the tarot in new ways.

It's important to have the symbols in front of you, so take out your deck and separate the major arcana. In most decks, these are the cards marked with a roman numeral at the top and a name at the bottom. The court cards—King of Wands, and so on—are not major arcana, so set them aside. Essentially, anything that does not contain the words "of wands," "of cups," "of disks," or "of swords" (or whatever your deck's equivalent suits are) is a major arcana card.

If you have a replica of an old deck, it may not have numbers at the top of the major arcana. And even if it does, those numbers may not correspond to what I have below. I will, therefore, refer to the cards by their names and numbers rather than their numbers alone. Also keep in mind that some decks change certain cards; you may need to consult the LWB to figure out which card is which. Also, the astrological and elemental attributions I'll list below are the most popular and derive from the Golden Dawn. Perhaps you use different ones. That's okay, as long as you understand how those other correspondences affect and change the meanings of the cards for you.

Memory works by association and grouping, so we will group these cards under their symbolic families. There are many ways to do this—for example, you could lay them out in two rows and make links between cards that fall in the same columns, or you could take out the Fool and break the rest of the deck into three sequential groups of seven. Those are all worthwhile activities for meditation and I recommend them as ways to understand the sequence of the cards and their relationships to each other. But the method I will use applies the keys of three, seven, and twelve (which we have not yet talked about) to the cards. As you can tell, this adds up to twenty-two, the number of major arcana cards in the deck.

Begin by going through the deck and taking out three cards: 0–The Fool, XII–The Hanged Man, and XX–Judgement. Lay the Fool, the Hanged Man, and Judgement out in front of you in that order. Remember that the quality of cardinality involves initiation and beginning, which the Fool also seems to indicate. The Hanged Man represents the quality of being fixed—permanence, stability, and focus. Finally, the quality of mutability involves sudden change, which describes Judgement pretty well, with its dead returning to life. Look again at each card, considering how each symbol on the card reflects something of the nature of the quality. For example, the Fool is chased by a dog and, in some decks, a crocodile, symbolizing that beginnings are often initiated by danger but at the same time, we have a companion (although in some decks, the dog is attacking the fool, which is another thing to consider—the beginnings sometimes separate us from our old companions, who tend to hold on). The Hanged Man is suspended, fixed, to a tree, but notice his facial expression. It is one of focused concentration, not pain. Spin such interpretations on each of the cards, making some notes in a journal. But do not rely on the notes: spend the majority of your intellectual energy focusing on the cards and linking the images on the cards to symbolic meanings in your head.

This process isn't an intellectual one. You should associate loosely and creatively. The goal is not to memorize the cards in the LWB, but to develop a relationship with the cards. Just as the best way to learn a language is not to memorize a long list of grammatical rules and vocabulary (contrary to the most popular method of teaching language in the United States, which is why most of us are monolingual), the best way to learn a divination system is not through rote memorization but by using the system to create meaning. These reorganizations serve as the first sentences you learn to actually use in a foreign language: "Hello, how are you?" You're shaking hands with the Anima Mundi, and the state of consciousness you find yourself in as you do this is the divinatory state of consciousness mentioned earlier.

On another occasion, or later if you still have time, take out the following four cards and place them under the Fool: IV–The Emperor, VII–The Chariot, XI–Justice, XV–The Devil. These four cards are symbolically associated with the four cardinal astrological signs of Aries, Cancer, Libra, and Capricorn. They do not themselves represent those signs, because their symbolism is in many ways much more complex—but there is a symbolic association. Each of the twelve signs is an interaction between quality and element, so we have the four elements represented here too: Aries is fire, Cancer is water, Libra is air, and Capricorn is earth. If the cardinal elements are those elements concerned with beginnings, creativity, and originality, we can derive a lot of meaning just by mixing the ideas of element and quality.

For example, the Emperor is the creative power of fire: authority. But at the same time, it's new or young: the Emperor can use that authority childishly. Similarly, the Chariot represents the creative power of water—it moves forward and transports us like a river. Justice is the creative power of air—reason and logic and fair judgment—all with the innocence of youth. The Devil is the creative power of earth—it can represent material success, but at the same time it gives us an immature view of the Earth in its image of chained humans who feel they cannot escape matter. Maybe you feel some of these interpretations are stretched, and that's fair. The only interpretations that will work for you are the ones you construct yourself, but they must be constructed on the foundation of sound symbolic thinking and a divinatory state of mind.

Now imagine that each of these cards is, in some way, linked with the Fool above it. For example, how can authority be a kind of Fool? How can the Devil? How can the driver of the Chariot? Such links do not need to be firm and completely convincing, but this exercise gives you practice in the key of complex cartomancy readings: the combination of symbols into a complex web.

Repeat this process, then, with the Hanged Man and the major arcana cards associated with the fixed quality, viz., Taurus, Leo, Scorpio, and Aquarius, respectively: V–The Hierophant, VIII–Strength, XIII–Death, and XVII–The Star. See how each of the elements of earth, fire, water, and air interact with the fixed quality of focused stability. You'll see how the Hierophant represents a focused power of earth: the stability of tradition. Strength is the kind that arises from energetic focus. Link these ideas with the images on the cards, and you'll find them easier to remember. Then, link them to the concept of the Hanged Man.

Finally, repeat this process again under Judgement, using the cards associated with the mutable signs of Gemini, Virgo, Sagittarius, and Pisces: VI–The Lovers, IX–The Hermit, XIV–Temperance, and XVIII–The Moon. These represent the unstable qualities of air, earth, fire, and water respectively. This instability isn't negative, merely undetermined and uncertain. So the Lovers represents an intellectual process of choice that hangs in the air, undetermined as of yet. The Hermit is the uncertainty of earth: the wanderer with no place, who spreads his wisdom to everyone. Temperance is the instability of fire, harnessed for change. For this reason, Aleister Crowley called it Art and reworked it to represent an alchemical transformation. The quantity of water represented in this image might strike you as odd for a card associated with fire—so that's worthy of some consideration. It's also worth noting that this figure is also unstable, one foot on land and one on the waves, just as the Anima Mundi is depicted in Fludd's diagram. Finally, the Moon represents the instability of water, the reflections and refractions of complex emotions. It is deception and concealment, but also dreams and fantasies.

The twelve cards of the zodiac, you may notice, fall conveniently into the traditional order of the twelve signs, so that if we lay out just those cards in their numbered order (at least as the Rider-Waite has it), we'll have the signs in their traditional order from Aries to Pisces.

Sign	Element	Quality	Card
Aries	Fire	Cardinal	Emperor
Taurus	Earth	Fixed	Hierophant
Gemini	Air	Mutable	Lovers
Cancer	Water	Cardinal	Chariot
Leo	Fire	Fixed	Strength
Virgo	Earth	Mutable	Hermit
Libra	Air	Cardinal	Justice
Scorpio	Water	Fixed	Death
Sagittarius	Fire	Mutable	Temperance
Capricorn	Earth	Cardinal	Devil
Aquarius	Air	Fixed	Star
Pisces	Water	Mutable	Moon

Once you get through these fifteen cards, you still may wonder how you can use this information for readings. After all, you see some relationships but don't really know, yet, what they mean in a way you can articulate as well as the LWB does. Now is a good time to play with some other arrangements of these fifteen cards. For example, rearrange the twelve cards associated with the zodiac into a new grid, one that groups together signs of the same elements. How do these groupings reveal new relationships? The fire cards, for example, are the Emperor, Strength, and Temperance. Does this triplet reveal anything if you read it as a story? "A person in authority must focus his or her strength to transform a situation." What of water? The Chariot, Death, and the Moon. Perhaps "Persistence in moving forward will end deception." Then again, you might say, "No, it means 'we are deceived if we think we can overcome death.'" Yes, it could also mean that, which is why flipping through a LWB for "the" meaning is useless if you wish to gain sophisticated oracles from the cards—or any other divination system. If, however, you are in a divinatory state of consciousness, one meaning will be clearer, truer, and more obvious than others.

You don't have the whole major arcana yet, but it might be fun to do a few test readings, just to stretch out your muscles a little before you have too much stuff to keep in mind. Take only these fifteen cards, shuffle them, and lay out a pair of cards. Now, try to interpret them as if they had arisen in a spread. Try to do this by intuition and by understanding the inevitable relationships between their symbols. For example, if you get the Hanged Man next to Temperance, is there a way that you can imagine the transformational powers of Temperance being focused by the Hanged Man's fixed sacrifice? If the Chariot and the Hierophant come together, how do they influence each other? The Chariot is enthusiastic and energetic, creative and forward-pushing, while the Hierophant is fixed. Is this pair indicative of a conflict between an urge to rush forward and try new things, against the weight of authority? Or is it a partnership? In truth, it depends on the situation and the intuitions of a reader in the appropriate state of mind.

We've got seven more cards to go, and if you predict that these are associated, traditionally (not a particularly old tradition, but tradition at least) with the seven planets, you'd be right on. Fish these cards out of the deck now, and lay them down in order. They are:

I–The Magician	Mercury
II–The High Priestess	Moon
III–The Empress	Venus
X–The Wheel of Fortune	Jupiter
XVI–The Tower	Mars
XIX–The Sun	Sun
XXI–The World	Saturn

It'd be just fabulous if these, like the cards associated with the signs, had the good grace to fall into the traditional order—but they don't. No worries: imprecision is the nature of language, and everything is a bit messy at the edges of any real language. And the neat and tidy order of the zodiacal arcana is somewhat artificial anyway, since that order was not fixed when Waite started making correspondences. He had some wiggle room, so he took it (swapping, for example, Justice and Strength to make the correspondence more obvious between Libra and Leo).

These correspondences do not really reflect a reality. The makers of the tarot probably did not—occult tradition and mystery notwithstanding—set out to encode all this astrological symbolism in the cards. Moreover, they didn't need to: the Anima Mundi did it nicely herself. If we search long enough, we can impose (or find, depending on your perspective) such symbolic associations in nearly any set of symbols. Here, we have people who did it with a card game, but we could do it with anything and therefore any set of symbols has the power to become an oracle, if we just learn to listen to it the right way.

That means that there's no objective message in the cards themselves. The message is in your relationship with the cards: again, meaning is the interaction of symbols in a mind. In order to finish building up the framework for that edifice of meaning, lay out the seven cards in order as shown above.

Consider how the quality of each of the planets is (or isn't) reflected in the cards. Obviously, the cards mean more than just their planets, or we could simply call the Tower "Mars" and be done with it. And you may notice symbols that strike you as odd or incongruous. These should not be ignored. Instead, they should lead to questions you can contemplate in a focused but relaxed way. For example, why is there a child on a horse in the Sun? How is the World related to constriction (Saturn)? It may help you to seek out some symbol of each of the planets in the trumps. If you're using a well-constructed deck, that shouldn't be hard. For example, the heart with the Venus symbol on it should remind you of Venus, and the other cards should fall into place, although some may be challenging (where is Mercury in the Magician? Well, Waite might say, who do you think is standing there?).

Now dig out the three quality cards, the Fool, the Hanged Man, and Judgement. Lay them out and place next to them each of the planetary cards in turn. What happens to the Magician when he is with the Fool? Is this the student, first learning his or her craft? What happens when you place him next to the Hanged Man? The fixed concentration of initiation. Next to Judgement: graduation and completion of a course of study. Now you can see how combinations can create more meanings than are available in the symbols alone.

The LWB isn't useless to you, but you could just throw it away if you want. You probably won't, though, and that's great. You'll find that you want to look up each of the cards again and see if you can figure out where the meanings come from. Now, when you read the LWB, the meanings that matter, that fit into your symbol system, will sit in your mind on the thrones of the symbolic associations you've already built. The ones that don't work for you won't. Memorizing the whole book will teach you what the author has in his or her brain. Letting the book roll through you and stick where it speaks to you will teach you what you have in yours.

CHAPTER VI

Getting in the Mood
and Getting Ready to Read

The key to divination is simply learning another way to listen. And just as when we listen to a friend talking, we have to listen to not just what's in front of us—the literal words—but also the context and unconscious communications that friend offers.

For example, if you're speaking with a friend who says "that's a nice car," you might decode the words literally: "I approve of an automobile that is nearby but not so close that I can touch it." Then you might notice that your friend has quirked one side of his mouth downward, and nodded his head to the side. You look to the side where your friend has gestured and see a beat-up old Pinto. You know that Pintos, even in their heyday, were not regarded as "nice," so you can modify your original interpretation to mean "look at that silly car; I can't believe anyone is driving it."

In this example, the literal meaning carried just the words "that's a nice car," and if that's all we had listened to, we'd have the wrong message. The nonverbal message consisted of a facial expression indicating derision, and a gesture directing where to look. The context indicated the car itself and your previous knowledge of that make and model. Without being aware of all of this, you cannot understand the full content of the message. The whole process is complicated by noise in the environment, as well.

In divination, the *literal meaning* is held in the system of divination itself—the meanings of the tarot or Lenormand cards. The *nonverbal meaning* consists of your insights and intuitions about how those meanings relate to the question. And the *context* is the querent's life situation, usually understood through the question but sometimes through conversation, as well as the cards that fall around the card you are reading. When any one of these channels of meaning is blocked, divination becomes more difficult. If a querent refuses to give you the question, a skilled reader knows that divination is still possible—but somewhat more difficult. Similarly, if you just read the meanings of the cards out of a book and do not employ intuition, you may end up with a somewhat satisfactory divination, but with much extraneous and useless material, and you may miss some of the more subtle connections. One might argue that psychic readers who just hold a querent's hand and answer questions are foregoing the entire literal meaning laid out by the symbols on the cards, but I've known some reputable psychic readers and they admit that symbolic images arise in their minds, which they read much as one might read the cards.[12] A reader might even build up a vocabulary of such things over time, knowing that a child with a ball, for example, indicates playfulness and not a literal child.

Noise is pollution of the channels with irrelevant messages, like when you're trying to talk to a friend in a public place and keep overhearing snatches of other people's conversation. Overall, noise can never be eliminated, just reduced. If reduced sufficiently, then communication can occur. In divination, reducing some kinds of noise is

---

12. This does not imply that this is the only legitimate way that such readers can read a person. I'm not making the claim that I have any idea how such things work, and since fakes widely outnumber legitimate readers, figuring it out is well beyond my limited patience.

easy: make sure nothing influences the randomness of your divination system (cards aren't stuck together, or missing) and define a careful question (which I will cover later). But we also sometimes have noise in our minds, which can interfere with our reading. Fortunately, eliminating this noise is also simple, but requires some meditational skills that most people rarely consciously learn.

The goal in meditation is not, contrary to what a lot of people say, to quiet the mind. A perfectly quiet mind would contain no messages at all. The goal is simply not to hold on to the mind as it runs around. If you're trying to listen to a friend in a coffee shop where lots of people are talking, you don't stand up and shout at everyone to shut up over and over. You learn to tune them out and let your friend's voice be the thing you concentrate on. In the case of divinatory listening, the annoying guy on his cell phone, the screaming child, the giggling teenagers are your conscious, everyday thoughts. One easy way to learn to shut them out (if not up) is as follows:

1. Start with the fourfold breath (inhale for a count of four, hold for a count of four, exhale for a count of four, repeat). If your body is tense or in pain, you will probably not be calm enough to hear your thoughts, and the first step to listening is hearing. If, as you relax, pain arises in your muscles, just allow it to arise. It's probably the release of tension that you're feeling, and if you just remain unafraid and allow yourself to notice the soreness of the tension that you hold throughout your day, it usually goes away. Don't be afraid that your body will come apart if you relax it; on the contrary, it'll fit together much better if you're not trying to hold it in by grim determination and stress alone.

2. Once you are relaxed, turn your attention to your thoughts. Let them arise without trying to control their speed, content, or number. Just look at each in turn briefly and identify it as a thought.

3. Do not judge a thought, either good or bad. Just look at it briefly, acknowledge it, and return to concentrating on your breath.

4. Another thought will arise, and another. Keep doing this for as long as you can—most teachers recommend a half hour or hour, but even five minutes a day is good practice.

5. The breakthrough is when you realize that your breath is just as interesting, if not more so, than any thought you might have.

The practice of this kind of meditation will inevitably make you calmer. You learn to see all your thoughts as contingent and largely unimportant. Or, at least, not worth clinging to. You may still have important thoughts—I like to think that once or twice a year I have a good one—but you no longer feel that every single notion is something you must cling to and judge. And freedom from judgment about your thoughts helps you see the truth of a situation. Instead of succumbing to fears or dwelling in unreasonable hope, you can experience both and still see that neither proves anything. Even without divination, this detachment can be useful.

The state of consciousness we achieve when we begin to divine is not rare or unusual. The Greeks called it *ekstasis*, "standing outside." It reflected the belief that this kind of trance let us step out of our bodies and gain perspective on reality. This kind of ecstasy is not something unusual; it's actually a common state of consciousness. Artists and creative people know it as "the zone" or a state of "flow," where ideas come easily and fit together intuitively. Most artists and writers know, however, that the best way to induce this state is to begin the creative activity. A writer may write for twenty or thirty minutes before entering a state of flow, and therefore writers often begin writing even before they're sure what they want to say.

Similarly, divination systems themselves help us to begin reading even before we achieve this necessary state of consciousness. We can help our minds get into the intuitive flow of consciousness by relaxing and letting go of our thoughts as described above. Eventually, you will be well-trained enough to fall into the state of divinatory consciousness just by shuffling the cards. It doesn't hurt, however, to have some additional quick tricks.

Movement can be meditation. Rhythmic rocking or even trembling can induce trance and maintain it, as Jan Fries explains in his excellent book *Seidways*.[13] Querents tend to be put off by rocking and trembling, unless they themselves practice magic. Still, when reading for yourself it's sometimes helpful to block out external stimulus and focus on the cards. I prefer a relatively slow—not headbanging but fast enough to be effective—rock back and forth, much like the movements of traditional Jews during davening prayer. It insulates me from external influences and focuses me on the cards.

Don't fear silence. This tip is an important one. Sometimes, especially when reading for a querent, we feel pressured to keep up a fluent stream of speech. Especially in American culture, we think that silence in social settings is a sign of a problem, and so we try to fill silence. However, divination is a kind of listening, and you cannot listen to someone while you talk nonstop to someone else. Don't fear long silences and don't try to fill the silence with speech just for the sake of saying something.

At the same time, **don't fear speaking.** This tip has two corollaries. First, don't be afraid to be wrong. If you see something and you're pretty sure it's there, tell the querent, and if they tell you are wrong, accept it (at least, outwardly—in my experience, querents do sometimes lie and then come back later and confess that I was right the first time). Also don't be afraid to give bad news, if you can do so with tact. Make sure you offer alternative interpretations if those are available. Better, don't be afraid to ask questions. Couching the bad news in the form of a question gives the querent more power and agency and emphasizes that divination is not destiny. The second corollary is that when reading for oneself, one should not be afraid to talk aloud. For years I couldn't figure out why I could read so much better for

---

13. Jan Fries, *Seidways: Shaking, Swaying, and Serpent Mysteries* (Oxford: Mandrake, 2009).

strangers than myself, then I realized that the only real difference was that I was talking aloud to strangers and not to myself. If we mean to translate one set of symbols to another, it helps to do so aloud. Even when I take notes on a reading, I now talk to myself. I figure, I do it in elevators and in my office, why not while divining?

Ritual. Ritual can also connect us to the source of divinatory wisdom. I frequently run into misconceptions about ritual. Usually the misconception is that ritual is a crutch or a stopgap, or even inherently harmful or distracting from what is important. Sometimes people say, "I'm not religious, but I'm spiritual" to mean "I don't do rituals, but I still have spiritual beliefs." In reality, everyone does rituals—countless rituals every single day. For example, the phrase "good morning" is a ritual. So is shaking hands, and at least part of your morning routine. Without ritual, living in society would be a challenge. Rituals reach out and link us to others. Pragmatically, the ritual phrase "how are you" means "I'm listening to you."

Part of the problem is a second misconception many people have about ritual, and that is that it involves robes, candles, expensive items, long incantations, and so on—and it can. But rituals can also be simple. The only real requirement of a ritual is that it be a repeated symbolic action.

I've written elsewhere about the way that a magician approaches ritual, so I'll just mention briefly that, while we might say, "Hello, how are you" or shake hands without giving it much thought, the magician approaches ritual mindfully. Even the simplest of rituals must be approached through all the senses. After all, as Giordano Bruno says in his treatise on mathematical magic:

> The animal ascends by the soul to the senses, by the senses into composite things, by the composite things into the elements, by the elements into the heavens, by

these into demons or angels, by these into God or divine grace.[14]

We begin, as animal or ensouled beings, to ascend with our rational souls, which engage the mixture of elements in the senses, and thus aspire to heaven.

Many diviners begin with prayer, either to one god or a particular deity of the divination. Israel Regardie suggests beginning tarot divinations with:

> I invoke thee, IAO, that thou wilt send HRU, the great angel that is set over the operations of this Secret Wisdom, to lay his hand invisibly upon these consecrated cards of art, that thereby we may obtain true knowledge of hidden things, to the glory of thine ineffable Name. Amen.[15]

Others prefer a more freeform prayer to the god of their choice. But ultimately, the prayer serves the purpose of announcing the diviner's desire to communicate. It is the "hello, how are you" of divination. The word "invoke" comes ultimately from the Latin verb *vocare*, meaning "to call." Beginning with an invocation of this nature calls out not only our intention to communicate, but also establishes as an act of faith that there is something to communicate with.

Ritual also includes actions, usually involving the medium of divination itself. There are enough rituals surrounding the tarot that you can take your pick. Some of those rituals are useful, such as the tradition of not allowing others to borrow the cards. It's important to maintain a sense of ownership. On the other hand, other rituals can hinder the effective use of the tarot, such as the superstition that one should never buy one's own tarot deck. The best rituals connect us

---

14. Giordano Bruno, *De Magia Mathematica*, http://www.esotericarchives.com/bruno/magiamat.htm (accessed August 13, 2010). Digital edition copyright 1999 by Joseph Peterson. My translation.

15. Israel Regardie, *The Golden Dawn* (St. Paul, MN: Llewellyn, 1989), 566-567.

with our method of divination, not separate us from it or throw up barriers between us and it.

The ritual I use for the tarot is a simple one. I mutter a prayer and then go through the cards one at a time, spending just a portion of a second on each. I make sure, however, to look at each and every card long enough to see its imagery. Ritual involves the senses, and so I activate each of the senses in turn. This procedure also has the benefit of giving me a chance to turn each card right-side-up if it isn't already. It also tunes me to the set of images that make up the symbol system of the tarot.

A longer, more elaborate ritual may be worthwhile at times, especially when you need to make an effort to get into a state of divinatory consciousness, perhaps because you have a lot of personal investment in the outcome of the question. Some readers set up special areas or tables, face certain directions, and so on—all worthwhile if you can afford the space.

For hints on creating rituals to connect us to the Anima Mundi, we can look back to the past.

One of the earliest forms of documented divination was *haruspicy*, the reading of an animal's internal organs. There is evidence that haruspicy began among the Babylonians, spread to the Etruscans, and then to the Romans. In all cases, although the symbol systems differed to some degree, the ritual remained similar: a priest cut open a sacrificial animal and examined its liver. It's easy to suppose that this was part of a simple quality control, first, and then later designed to communicate with the gods. However, it's also easy to imagine making the step between offering food to the gods—and sharing in it—in a ritual fashion, and speaking to the gods. In other words, haruspicy bridges communion and communication.

In this case, the ritual involved a traditional Roman sacrifice: the animal had to come to the altar willingly, was often sprinkled with wine or mead, and—after prayers—was killed quickly and relatively humanely. The haruspex (priest) then examined the entrails, both to determine if the sacrifice was acceptable and to check for signs of disease. The animal was roasted and then shared in a sort of large communal barbecue. Some of us may be a bit squeamish about this, but the typical Roman ate mostly meat sanctified in this manner.

Nearly every other form of divination, from observation of birds to the incubation of dreams, practiced by ancient Romans and Greeks involved a sacrifice and a prayer. In light of this ritual outline, we can create a ritual of any complexity we desire: first, the offering establishes mutual obligation between human and divine intelligence. Then, the human offers an act of communication. The sense of mutual obligation created by the gift assures a response. We don't need to slaughter animals to achieve this same dynamic system. For one thing, it'll get our cards all messy. But we can put on a bit of incense, pour out a small offering, or light a candle—rituals of sacrifice that anyone of any religious persuasion can do without making the living room an abattoir.

A ritual can be simple, but picking up a system of divination— even just listening to your body—isn't taking out the trash. It's an act that deserves full attention. In fact, it *is* an act of attention: attention to the patterns that make up our lives. Ritual can help us listen to those patterns more carefully.

No matter what means we use, it's important to begin by becoming ready to listen—by silencing the noise in our minds and in our environment, and attending to the subtler messages of the cards.

CHAPTER VII

Preparing to Tell the Story

Reading the tarot and reading the Petit Lenormand are similar activities. Create a question, select cards, lay them out, and make up a story. The details may differ, but that is always the basic outline of the procedure.

The questions most suited to divination are those that uncover meaning rather than data—that put together stories that relate to the readers rather than give them disconnected bits of information. So if a querent asks who stole their lunch at work, you as a reader should recognize first that this is a convergent question, one asking for a single datum, but that there is a story behind it. Most readers would simply lay out the cards and offer a description of the thief, which may or may not work if the querent does the hard work of creating meaning himself or herself. The diviner, however, might go a bit further and ask some questions designed to elicit meaning and revise the querent's original question. First, the diviner should question the presupposition. "Why do you imagine someone stole the lunch rather than other possibilities?" While the querent explains, the diviner needs to watch for emotional connections and try to understand the network of meanings surrounding work. Let's imagine this scenario:

Q: Who stole my lunch at work? *Initial question seeking data.*

D: Why do you think the lunch was stolen? *Question encouraging querent to create context.*

Q: I didn't eat it, and it went missing. *Still a data-based answer.*

D: How often do people at work steal from other workers? *Resisting the urge to question the querent's interpretation of events, the diviner seeks context. The diviner frames the question in specific, meaning-constructing terms rather than as a yes/no question.*

Q: All the time, with me! *The diviner notices that the querent seems both angry and sad.*

D: You seem angry and sad. *Reflecting the querent's apparent emotions helps the querent introspect and feel safe.*

Q: I am. I mean, why does no one respect me at work? *The querent has moved from a convergent question to a divergent one—from one that seeks a simple answer to one that creates meaning and has many potential answers.*

D: I don't know. Let's ask the cards why it seems no one respects you at work. *The diviner refines the question a bit to include the possibility that the querent is imagining the disrespect, but otherwise goes with the querent's question.*

A psychologist confronting the same question would approach it differently. But a diviner isn't a psychologist and shouldn't try to be one. (If you're going to read for a living, it's a good idea to make up some cards with emergency numbers on them, including professional psychologists and the like whom you can recommend.) The goal for the diviner is to help the querent arrive at the real question that matters.

During the mercifully short time that I gave readings for money, it always amazed me when people would go to the trouble of finding me (I didn't advertise), scheduling a reading, and paying the fifty bucks, and then have no idea what they wanted to know. "Do you have a question?" I'd ask. "Um, I don't know."

I quickly learned that what they meant wasn't that they had no question, but that they genuinely didn't know how to formulate the question. First, they weren't sure if I'd think their question was worthy; they were afraid that this dorky young man at his kitchen table was going to criticize their life choices. Second, they simply didn't know what kind of questions the tarot could answer. Sometimes they'd say, "I have a question, but do I have to tell you?" I'd tell them that I could divine their answer but it would be easier and clearer if I knew the question, and even if they didn't tell me, I'd find out the question during the process of divination. Often, they'd start with their question a secret, and halfway through the reading they'd reveal it themselves, usually by visibly steeling themselves for the imagined embarrassment to come, then blurting it out.

Other times, querents would come with questions and it would become obvious about a third of the way into the reading that they really wanted to know something else. Again, there were emotional barriers preventing them from admitting, perhaps even to themselves, what they wanted to know. But at other times, they simply wouldn't know how to ask a question.

No question that drives someone to seek out a tarot card reading and pay a significant amount of money is inappropriate. But sometimes querents are not ready to own their questions, and sometimes don't know themselves what their questions really are. Knowing how to ask a question is itself an art, even in mundane settings. Professionals such as lawyers, teachers, and psychologists spend long hours in training to learn to ask questions. However, each of them learns a different kind of question. Lawyers focus on convergent questions, or questions that have clear, specific, factual answers: "Where were you on March 3?" Teachers mingle convergent questions with divergent questions, those without clear, factual answers, such as "why did the Civil War start?" And psychologists often focus on introspective questions: "Why do you believe that no one loves you?" So the type of question is tailored to the purpose. Lawyers wish to make the facts of a case clear to a jury. Teachers wish students to think about complex events. And psychologists want patients to learn to think about themselves in a more nuanced way.

What sorts of questions, then, are appropriate for divination? The main idea to keep in mind, and perhaps one of the most important ideas in this book, is this: *Divination does not reveal data; it helps create meaning.*

Data are the answers to convergent questions. A convergent question usually begins with "what," "who," or "where" or is a yes/ no question, although not every yes/no question or question beginning with one of these words is convergent. All possible answers to a convergent question are data; a datum is a piece of information that can be observed to be factual or nonfactual. If you list out all possible answers to a convergent question, only one of them will be "right." For example, "Who took my pudding?" I can make a list of everyone who might have taken my pudding:

John Smith took my pudding.
Susie Smith took my pudding.
John Jones took my pudding.
and so on. . . .

Ultimately, I would end up with a list of every single person on earth, and I could cross off people as I found out that they didn't take my pudding. If my list was complete, I'd end up with a single name, the guilty party who took my pudding. Of course, no one answers convergent questions this way, but the principle is the same: of all items that could answer the question, only one is acceptable. These factual and exclusive answers are data.

Meaning is the way data fit together into a pattern. So I might ask "Why did John Jones take my pudding?" Now, there are multiple possible answers, and I would hard-pressed to provide a complete list of possibilities, let alone narrow it down to one observable and verifiable fact. The divergent questions that create meaning usually begin with "why" and "how," although some yes/no questions also qualify, although those that do usually contain a "why" or a "how" within them. For example, "Am I ever going to make more than $40,000 a year?" This seems like a yes/no question, and thus is convergent, but in reality a querent asking you this really wants to know *how* to make that target income, and not whether or not he or she will. Answering this question, then, involves answering both the convergent part (yes) and also the unspoken divergent part (by doing such and such).

The trick is identifying what the querent is really asking, especially when the querent is asking a convergent question at first. A good reader will help the querent formulate a meaning-seeking rather than a data-seeking question. A meaning-seeking question may provide some data to the querent, but the important part, and the thing that divination excels at, is the creation of meaning. If a querent can come away saying "I understand" rather than "I know," you have accomplished your job as a reader.

We don't always have querents. Sometimes we read for ourselves, even though many readers (of tarot or of other methods of divination) find it difficult. First, there's the issue of separating oneself from the desired outcome. It's sometimes hard not to read our wishful thinking—or just as often, if not more so—our worries into the symbols of the divination system. Second, no one is there to force us to formulate the question clearly when we read for ourselves. It is essential to work on the question before you do the divination, to move it toward a more meaning-centered rather than data-centered question.

The single best way to do this is to write the question. Do you resist this suggestion? Is your resistance growing out of the same emotional resistance as a querent who does not want to say his or her question aloud? If so, why do you have that emotional resistance? Look at why you don't wish to own this question: probably, it's a perfectly acceptable question and you don't wish to own it because you don't wish to accept the implication of any question—namely, that you do not know the answer. Asking is an admission of ignorance.

Ignorance isn't a vice. It's the necessary condition for knowledge: ignorance mingled with curiosity creates learning. If we were never ignorant, we could never learn and without learning we could never grow. Growth frightens people, because it involves rejecting some part of ourselves or admitting that something we once did or was no longer will work. Insofar as divination helps us overcome that initial fear of admitting ignorance, it encourages growth and positive change. If divination addressed data rather than meaning, it would never engage such fears. Few people are fearful of data, unless they can place that data into a meaningful structure.

Data in a meaningful structure is understanding. Once we understand something, we have gained some power over it. The word "comprehend," a synonym of understanding, implies such overcoming in its etymology. It comes from roots meaning "to grasp or seize completely." That doesn't mean that understanding banishes fear. No one is afraid of mere data: the height of Kilimanjaro doesn't matter to most people, one way or another, other than as a fact. However, if you have to climb it, suddenly that number might instill some apprehension. Interestingly, "comprehend" and "apprehend" both come from the same root: to seize something. When we seize the fact and place it into a meaningful structure, we comprehend it. When the meaningful structure seizes us, we are apprehensive.

Divination therefore doesn't banish fear or cure all ills. It merely helps us make meaning from fact. This "merely" is large enough, though, to make divination worthwhile.

To say "divination is good at meaning, and not at uncovering data" might be seen as disingenuous. After all, it neatly answers the skeptic's sneer that, if one can divine the future, why not simply divine the future lottery numbers and become rich. Or, more seriously, why not determine the timing of great national tragedies and disasters, and warn the applicable people. First, while it's possible to divine such facts as lottery numbers, it's possible only when those facts have been placed into a meaningful structure. For most people, winning the lottery isn't real; it's at best a dream or fantasy. Second, and more importantly, psychics do sometimes try to warn people of coming disasters. They're rarely listened to.

Let me give you two instances. The first was during the Persian Gulf War of 1990. I was in high school at the time, and I was experimenting with divination in dreams. I also had family members involved in the war. One night in August shortly after the war started, I received a startling dream in which my mother shouted upstairs that my cousin, currently fighting in the Gulf, would be home on a particular day in March. At this point, most people expected the war to take some time, and when I mentioned to other people with family in the Gulf that the war would be over by March, they mostly did not believe me. I had to be easy to dismiss. I was a strange little kid, as you might well imagine.

My cousin earned my everlasting annoyance by missing his flight home and coming home on the day after I predicted. I still count this as a successful divination of fact, but the fact mattered to me. It wasn't merely a date (and I forget the date, although I suppose I could dig it out of my magical diary of the time, if I could wade through the tedious teenage angst). It was a date placed into a system of knowledge.

The second is a date anyone should have been able to predict. But on September 10, 2001, all I knew is that I was having a bad day. Ten minutes before a class, my pants split. Right up the seat. I had to cancel class and go home to change. I only hoped that people would forget my humiliation.

The next day, a Tuesday, was a day off for me. I lazed around the house for the afternoon, then decided to walk down to the record shop and buy a new CD. I browsed for a good long while, half-listening to something that sounded like some experimental performance art, a fake news report of some kind. Finally, as I was checking out (and I still remember which CD I bought, as well as that I listened to it obsessively for weeks afterwards in a sort of fugue state), I asked the bearded guy behind the counter if that was real news, because the phrase "crashed an airplane into the Pentagon" had finally filtered through my oblivious consciousness.

I first heard of the 9/11 attacks from an aged hippy at a record store while buying a Butthole Surfers' CD.

Now, why didn't that fact appear in my dreams? Surely it would mean something to me, as it did to every American. Why didn't I dream about that disaster? Perhaps because I was distracted by my bad day, or maybe for other reasons.

And yet, because of this event, I will never forget my trivial embarrassment, which otherwise probably would have faded into the past like every other silly thing I have no doubt done but since forgotten. I do remember that day because it has become anchored to an event of greater meaning. Similarly, as a man who likes music, I have bought many, many CDs. The only one I remember buying in all its detail is the one I bought that day. It is anchored, for better or worse, in that day of monumental and traumatic change.

I don't tell the story above because it is amusing. I also am not making light, by any means, of what happened on September 11, 2001. People of the generation before mine used to say, "Where were you when JFK was shot?" And they remembered, because of that anchoring.

That's the point: precognition works a bit like memory. Those things with anchors, with meaning, no matter how trivial they may seem to others, stay with us in our memory. Similarly, those things with anchors in the future are more likely to cast shadows back. September 11 has cast a long shadow over my and many other people's memories. Why did it not cast a shadow back into the past?

Frankly, I don't know. I suspect because I didn't ask the right question. If my daily divination was "what will tomorrow hold for me?" I might see a day off, some shopping, and some sadness. I might wonder what the sadness was, but never find out that it was actually something much greater than my personal sadness, because I would never think to ask, "What will tomorrow hold for America?" Moreover, I have never been to New York. I had no anchors already in place until that attack occurred. But none of these explanations satisfy me, and probably don't satisfy you. Still, perhaps we can keep thinking about it and maybe find a theory that fits eventually.

I venture that most of my readers do not remember the height of Kilimanjaro, even though almost everyone has probably, at one time or another, seen or heard of it. However, if any of them have climbed Kilimanjaro, or are mountain climbers, or interested in geography or geology, that number may roll out of their mind as easily as their phone number. I can recite lots of poetry from memory, not because of any innate talent or ability, but because I read a lot of it and it matters a great deal to me. It would be easy for a skeptic to say, "Sure, divination only works with stuff that matters, rather than easily verifiable data. That's convenient." But few skeptics say the same about memory. Surely memory would be easier to study if people would conveniently memorize numbers, but they don't. They memorize what those numbers mean to them.

This link between memory and foreknowledge also helps explain the appeal of the tarot and Lenormand. Both decks feature images similar to those used in memory systems, especially medieval memory systems, in which one memorizes a series of images or ideas by rote, and then uses those as anchors for other, new ideas one wishes to learn. These anchor images were called *loci*. Perhaps the cards are the loci for the memory of the Anima Mundi.

In reading for yourself, you need to do the same thing as we did with the querent at the beginning of this chapter, but alone. Write out your question and work out what meaning you are seeking before even touching a divination system. For one thing, you may find you don't really need to do a divination at all. But more importantly, you'll find the real question that matters for you. Introspection is a bit harder than examining a querent in front of you, so I recommend a method called focusing, which isn't a divination system itself, but is useful in divining.[16]

A full account of focusing would fill this book and then some, but in its simplest form, it's asking your body to respond to ideas. For

---

16. This is a technique originally developed for therapists by Eugene Gendlin, a professor at the University of Chicago. There are several good introductions on focusing readily available. One of my favorites is Ann Weiser Cornell, *The Power of Focusing: A Practical Guide to Emotional Self-Healing* (Oakland, CA: New Harbinger, 1996).

example, if you have a problem that requires divination, you can focus on the physical or quasiphysical sensations caused by contemplating that problem, and use them as a compass to point you to the question to divine on.

The process is simple:

1. Relax in a comfortable position, either sitting or lying down. There should be no particular strain on any part of your body, and you should loosen any tight clothing.

2. Hold the problem you wish to divine about in your mind. At this point, do not think of it as a question. Instead, let your mind scan your body until you find a bodily sensation that seems to correspond to the problem. This is easier to do than to describe.

3. Focus your attention on that bodily sensation. It may intensify at first. Ask it, "What are you?" Let answers arise and test each one by comparing the feeling to your description. If the feeling lessens or changes, you've hit on it. The descriptions may not make much conscious sense. It could be as simple as "are you anger?" or as complex as "are you the feeling of being abandoned in a dangerous place by people you trusted?" Be patient. There might an urge to find the "right" label early, but keep testing until you feel a definite and notable change in the feeling. That's the right label.

4. Still focusing on the sensation, ask, "What sort of question would enlighten me on this problem?" Wait until a question arises and test it against the feeling. Again, if the feeling lessens or changes, you know you've hit upon a good question. If not, then keep trying.

5. It can help to write questions down and see them objectively; it can intensify that feeling of "rightness" or "fit" that comes.

Let's imagine I wish to gain information about my financial situation. Perhaps I'm worried about it. First, I relax in my comfy chair, the unsung magical tool of all true wizards. Then I think about money and pay attention to my body. Perhaps I feel a sort of fluttering in my stomach. I focus on this and it intensifies a bit. "Are you fear?" I ask, and it does nothing as I hold it gently in my attention. "Are you anger, maybe that I'm not making enough money?" It does not react. "Are you excitement?" Suddenly, the fluttering sensation increases and darts upwards a bit toward my heart. I'm on the right track. "Are you excitement at the possibilities of using my money for something?" Again, the fluttering changes, this time to a comfortable warm feeling. I've found it. Now I ask, "What kind of question would best enlighten me in regards to my financial situation?" I make a few notes on a pad of paper while keeping my attention on the warm feeling. "Where can I find a source of new income?" Nothing. "Should I ask for a raise?" Nothing. "How can I best invest my savings to optimize their value?" Suddenly, the warm feeling spreads throughout my chest and face. I know I've hit on it. I always like to end a focusing session by thanking my body for being willing to communicate. Then I get up and prepare the divination.

Focusing ensures that you find questions that matter, because a good question matters both to your mind and your body. We have intellectual notions about what sorts of questions to ask, but in reality it's the question that affects you—all of you—that has the best chance of being answered accurately. And perhaps I'd get the lottery numbers from my divination, but probably, just because of the nature of the financial world, I'd get other more useful advice. If I had sat down right away and asked either a vague question—"What am I going to do about my financial situation?"—or a specific but meaningless data question—"Will I be able to afford a new garage door?"—I'd probably not end up with as useful an answer as if I sought a truly meaningful question. After all, once I determine how to invest my savings, I can easily see what I'm going to do about my financial situation and if I can afford a new garage door.

Many diviners offer suggestions about appropriate questions, such as avoiding "should" questions, that are all good advice. But I think you'll find that you naturally follow such advice by keeping in mind the principle that a question must be meaningful to both your mind and body. A "should" question usually arises from fear. Similarly, gossipy questions, which most readers won't answer, really have at their root an uncertainty about the querent's place in his or her social networks. Getting at these root questions is the true foundational skill of a good diviner, even more so than being able to read the symbols of his or her divination system.

Salience and Story

Take out either your Lenormand deck or your tarot deck and shuffle it, asking, "What do I need to know in my exploration of the tarot and Lenormand?" Lay out the cards in a single row of three cards. Look carefully at what you've laid out: what card leaps out to you, without your necessarily realizing why? That card is salient. Push it up a little higher above the line of the other two cards. You've created a new pattern: a triangle, if it was the middle card, or a slope if it was one of the other two cards. What does that shape suggest to you in regards to your story about the cards? How do the other two cards fit into that story? Don't even think about what the cards are supposed to mean: just try to link them into a story that relates to your experiences with the tarot and Lenormand.

In making this story, you are reading the cards. You are listening to what the Anima Mundi is telling you.

The real skill of any divination system isn't manipulating cards. The real skill is to listen. And this listening occurs, as I've written before, in the divinatory state of consciousness, a relaxed state of calm and alertness similar to hypnosis or the "alpha state." But what are we listening for? Two things: salience and story.

Salience is simply what sticks out. If you're reading an astrological chart, it might be tempting just to cut and paste the paragraphs describing the various relationships between the planets, signs, and houses. I had such a computer program once. It'd calculate the chart and write up a seven- or eight-page report on the chart that was, essentially, gibberish. Where it wasn't full of Barnum statements

(statements that are true for nearly everyone, like "although you enjoy people, sometimes you would prefer to be alone") it was full of downright contradictions. It's no wonder then that skeptics scoff especially hard at astrology.

What the computer lacked was the ability to intuit salience. The skill of intuiting salience is universal throughout humanity, though. We do it every time we notice something out of place. If you've ever invited someone over, then glanced around and noticed how messy your house is, then you've made the empty pop cans, the papers, and dust salient. We do something similar with divination, but instead of inviting a coworker over for coffee, we notice salience because we've invited the Anima Mundi over to talk.

A tarot card reader has a lot of flexibility. For example, a reader using the Rider-Waite deck might draw the Moon when asked about a relationship. The obvious book-definition is "you're being deceived," which is nice and succinct and fair. But look for a moment at the card, and let your eye fall wherever it may. In that case, my eye falls on the rocks near the path. And I think of rocks as symbolic of obstacles, but the path goes on. Now, I can give more insight: "Deception is a real problem at this stage in your relationship, but it's not too late to work through it." Your eye might fall elsewhere on the card, leading to a different meaning.

In seeking salience in your readings, trust is paramount. Let your eye roam over the card or the spread until it "sticks," and then trust that this sticking place is relevant to the reading. Work it in to your interpretation or ask the querent about it, but do not ignore it. Sometimes, these images will evoke other, related images in your mind. In that case, add those to the reading as well, using the overt meanings of the cards as guides but trusting the salience of what arises in your mind as you read.

The second element to effective divination, story, is the ability to link symbols together into narrative. Narrative is the way that we understand our experiences. We place them into a life story and give them meaning in context of the whole story. For example, certain restaurants are not just where I ate dinner a few times: they're connected with the person I love and our story together. Similarly, the symbols on the tarot cards or the Lenormand cards are all parts of a story. Some are setting, some are plot, and some are characters. Telling which is which isn't as difficult as it might seem.

Symbols of setting tell us where things are occurring. Sometimes you can simply assume that, and sometimes it's determined by the place a card falls in a spread, as I'll discuss in the next chapter. A lot of wands in a tarot reading or the presence of 14–Fox in the Lenormand probably mean that the setting is at work. A lot of cups or 4–House, at home. Pentacles often indicate places of business, education, and commerce (as does 19–House), or familial estates. Swords can be any unpleasant place, including any of the above.

Symbols of plot tell us conflicts and strategies for overcoming them. Swords are a natural for depicting conflicts and obstacles, but every card—even the "good" ones—can. After all, the Nine of Cups is a pretty positive card, but someone suddenly getting his or her heart's desire is the plot of many a story—and it rarely ends well.

Finally, characters are those who act things out. Traditionally, the court cards depict characters involved in your story, but any card can in practice. The Magician might indicate someone skilled whom you consulted to help you out. The Seven of Swords might indicate someone who is too clever for his or her own good, and so on. In the Lenormand, those cards containing king and queen insets can also stand for people, as explained earlier.

All of this holds true for other divination systems as well, and keeping an intuitive eye out for characters, setting, and plot—or just trying to link the symbols together into a story—is really all that's asked of a reader. Once you begin to link symbols across cards and find relationships in context, suddenly meanings multiply and you have a full language. Unlike natural languages, this symbolic language is the language of the unconscious, and the native tongue of the Anima Mundi and the individual Genius.

Dangers

Magic and magical practices are real, and therefore have real effects. I believe that magic is beneficial and divination can help improve lives, but at the same time there are real dangers to any magical practice. These dangers rarely take the form of ravening demons or secret evil cults, which might be a disappointment to those of us who are fans of contemporary fantasy novels. But that doesn't make them unreal.

The first and greatest danger is deception. Any magical operation designed to gather information can also be used to hide information or dissemble. A quick glance at the yellow pages will find pages of psychics in most large cities, and while some are legitimate, many have no particular interest in helping people. These psychics are the ones who will play to a querent's desire to feel special, telling them that they are important in some cosmic sense and—inevitably—the target of some powerful evil that, fortunately, the psychic can avert. The psychic will charge grossly inflated prices for ordinary supplies, which have been "specially blessed." Or, in one variation of the scam, the psychic will tell the querent that his or her money is cursed and must be cleansed in a complex ritual. The confidence artist instructs the querent to withdraw his or her money from the bank in cash, wrap it in a special cloth, and bury it or perform some other ritual that takes it out of sight for enough time for the artist to leave town. Through simple sleight of hand, the confidence artist has swapped the bundle of money for an identical one of cut newspaper. When the querent opens the bundle, he or she discovers that, indeed, the money was not so cursed that the confidence artist wouldn't take it.

Cold reading, the practice of many fake psychics, is simple enough to learn and to avoid. It consists of making a large number of shotgun predictions, and elaborating on those that get a response. Since people have a tendency not to notice errors and to exaggerate the effectiveness of hits, a credulous querent can be taken in by a cold reading. Many television psychics, especially those claiming to speak to dead relatives, are actually practicing cold reading, made easier by their ability to edit out the misses and keep in the hits. One of the cues you are dealing with a cold reader is their ability to find facts that are essentially meaningless. Ironically, those readers who deal in easily identifiable data are more likely to be fake than real. After all, as I mentioned earlier, divination is better at creating meaning than finding specific, disconnected facts. Anyone who is finding those specific data about one's life, especially the impressive trivial things that TV psychics specialize in, is probably finding them through other, more mundane, fraudulent means.

There's also the moral danger of doing readings for others. It's easy to fall into the trap of telling querents what they want to hear, just for the warm glow of approval. Giving good news feels good, even if it's not true. On the flip side, you can always justify brutal honesty as a commitment to the truth, when it's really just a streak of sadism. If you are going to learn to read for others, develop tact. It's also important to be certain of your divination before you offer advice. And never offer medical or legal advice—American laws jealously protect those fields from encroachment.

The other danger of deception is that of self-deception. If it's easy to tell a querent what he or she wants to hear, it's even easier to tell yourself what you want to hear. And it's also easy to be sadistic toward yourself, and confirm fears and worries over and over again. Both of these forms of self-deception arise when we use divination as a means of reassurance rather than information-gathering. Reassurance doesn't sound so bad, but in reality it can be pernicious. Seeking reassurance, from the cards or even just from others, can actually reinforce worries and encourage procrastination. In divination, it runs counter to the entire purpose: to gain true answers.

You are using divination for reassurance if you ask the same question over and over again. Also, if you notice yourself rejecting or disliking a particular reading because it doesn't match what you want it to say, you're in danger of training your mind away from finding the truth. Similarly, if you find that all of your readings are gloomy and depressing, you may well need to put aside the divination system for a while and work on your own mind. Eventually, if you keep this up, you'll train the Anima Mundi not to tell you the truth, and then the true value of the system of divination will be corrupted. Ultimately, divination requires integrity.

The other danger, obsession, relates to reassurance, but is more fundamental. Obsession involves consulting a divination system before making even ordinary decisions. Some diviners do a short divination for each day. An obsessive, however, will divine for every single decision of that day. "Shall I go to the store and buy milk? Should I go to that party tonight?" The motivation here is the same as above: worry. After all, going to the store is inconsequential, unless you suspect that there's some danger. And if you feel like going to a party, you should go. These aren't hard choices unless behind them are questions like "if I go to the store and buy milk, will I get hit by a bus on the way?" and "if I go to that party, will I be humiliated in public?" The desire to plan out an entire life in advance is not conducive to living a good one, and if magic is about anything, it's about living a good life.

It's easy to tell if you're obsessing. If you begin a lot of your divinatory questions with "should," you may be expressing unstated worries. Also, you may find that you're having trouble reading the response to your query, because it's really addressing the underlying concern. Some divination systems will even tell you when you're being obsessive or asking the wrong question. The key here is to address the underlying worry, either through therapy, mindfulness, or acceptance.

It's not all grim and gloomy. If you trust a con artist, you'll lose money; that's obvious and has nothing much to do with magic. If you use divination systems to tell you what you want to hear, eventually you won't be able to use them to get real information. But even that isn't a permanent state. Eventually, you can train yourself out of your obsession or need for reassurance. The benefits of divination outweigh the possible dangers.

CHAPTER VIII

Some Tarot Spreads

Meaning comes from relationships between symbols in the mind. One important set of symbols is the context of the question itself. If someone asks about love, and you draw the Lovers, the card means something very different from what it means if someone asks about business success. In love, a partnership with emotional overtones is a good thing. In business, however, such a relationship could lead to problems.

Another kind of context used in most systems of divination is that of the spread or template. This template divides up the life of the querent analytically, so that the cards can take additional meaning from context.

The simplest spread is the single-card reading. In the single-card reading, all the context is provided by intuition. The card is only a spark. This means the single-card reading is a bit of an advanced exercise, but a good one. It forces you to lean on your intuition and to rely on the divinatory state of consciousness. There are several books that list various questions you might ask, and the meaning of a single card in response. This approach is a bit more mechanical than necessary, but it does illustrate the role of context.

The more cards we lay out, the more associational meaning we can intuit from their combinations. If we draw one card, the context exists only in our mind, because there are only 78 possible cards we might draw from a full tarot deck. If we draw two cards, the context exists not only in our mind, but between those two cards, and there are now 6,006 (78 x 77) possible combinations of cards we might draw, and if we draw three cards, we suddenly have a large number of possible combinations of symbols (456,456 of them, 78 x 77 x 76). This is a lot of potential context, now not only in the mind of the reader and querent, but on the table itself. It's not always the case that the more combinations of symbols the better, and too much complexity can be confusing. Extremely large card spreads can paralyze the imaginations of inexperienced readers. For them, it's often wise to start small. But within reason, the more patterns that become available, the easier it is to enter the state of consciousness that makes associational reasoning possible.

Specific Spreads for the Tarot

The simplest tarot spread is the one-card spread, but how much space can I take to describe drawing a single card?

A more useful spread for most questions, and the workhorse that gets about 90 percent of my questions answered, is the three-card spread.

1. Shuffle your cards according to your preferred ritual and draw three cards off the top, laying them from left to right on the table in front of you.

2. Look at the middle card. That's the main theme. Fit it to your question: what answers does it imply?

3. Once you have a few broad strokes laid out, look to its left and right, to fine-tune what it says.

For example, you ask, "What do I need to know about my coworker Mary?" and you draw three cards at random from the major arcana and arrive at the Magician, the Tower, and the Hanged Man. The Tower is the central card, and Mary's theme: she is undergoing some hard times, it seems. What sorts of hard times? Ones arising out of a lack of skills and talents. These hard times paralyze her: she's unable to move. The cards change meaning if rearranged; if we put the Hanged Man in the center, we now have a woman undergoing an initiation which will gain her new skills, even as it tears away old edifices.

Let's try another example. I ask the cards, "How can I quickly and successfully finish the book of poetry I'm working on?" I draw three cards—hold on, let me go get my deck—and end up with the Empress, the Hanged Man, and Temperance. The theme card is the Hanged Man, which counsels stillness. So that seems to indict the "quickly" part of my question: "You can't do it both quickly and well," it seems to say. The Empress reminds me that many of these poems are love poems and must be genuinely felt, not merely faked. They have to grow naturally out of real experience. Finally, Temperance is the card that Crowley renamed Art: here, it seems to suggest mixing and matching. It seems to suggest that perhaps some fragments and partially finished poems could be combined into new poems.

Nonce Spreads

The three-card method of reading can be detailed and efficient despite the low number of cards. As I said, most of the times I consult the tarot I use this method. I also sometimes create what I call nonce spreads: spreads I just make up as I need them. Say I want to know which of two choices would lead to better results. I'll ask, "What will be the result if I do such-and-such?" and "What will be the result if I do this other thing?" I draw three cards for each choice and lay them out in front of me. I read each of them as a hypothetical story tracing out the likely results of making each decision. Alternately, I might label a particular set of triplets pros and another cons, and read them that way.

The method for doing this is not as intimidating as it might seem. You simply need to divide up your question into parts.

1. Begin by writing out your question, as explained in the previous chapter, in as much detail as you can.

2. Circle every noun and verb in the question you have laid out. Nouns, as you recall, are words that describe objects, including people. Verbs describe actions.

3. Lay out a card for every noun and verb that seems significant to you. You may also lay out clarifying cards where they seem appropriate.

4. If your question begins "how" you can lay out cards for "advice" and "warning," as well. If it begins "why," you can lay out cards for levels of cause—surface cause, deeper psychological cause—or effects, as seems appropriate. For "option" questions, I lay out separate cards for each option.

For example, if I ask, "How can I get that promotion at work?" I identify one verb—get—and three nouns: "I," "Promotion," and "work." So I lay out four cards—one for my position, one for the action of getting the promotion, one for the promotion itself, and one for the work environment. I may also lay out some clarifying cards based on the type of question: a card for advice, what I should do; and a card for warning, what I should not do.

Procedures

With the major arcana alone, you're limited in the sizes of your spreads somewhat. But even with only twenty-two cards, you can get some significant detail using a reading procedure rather than a spread. A procedure differs from a spread in that it doesn't impose a layout or a set meaning to the card positions. It might also include several different ways of reading the cards in one throw.

I've created a simple procedure for the major arcana below, loosely based on the long and detailed Golden Dawn method of reading the cards. If you're interested in the full method, it can be found online in several places, as well as in Israel Regardie's *Golden Dawn.*[17]

1. Begin by shuffling your cards according to your usual ritual.

2. Ask a question about a particular situation, then pull off the top card and set it to the left-hand side. This card is the "one card" answer to your question, or the overall theme card.

3. Now deal the remainder of the cards into three rows of seven cards each. The top row is the past; the middle the present; and the bottom row is the future. Or you could rebrand the rows for some questions: let the top be the plot, the middle row the characters, and the bottom row the setting.

4. The first card in each row is that row's theme card. Combine the theme card's meaning with the overall theme card to get an overview.

5. Now it gets tricky. *You won't read every card*; just the ones pointed to by the theme cards and subsequent relevant cards. Use the table below to count from the theme card to lead to another card, which you'll also read, tying it to the question and the theme, as well as the meaning of the pack.

6. From that card, count to the next, and so on.

7. When you get to the end of the line, just keep counting from the beginning again, until you land on a card you've already read. Always count the first card as one (so if the top row's theme card is the Fool, you'll count it as one, the next card as two, and the card after it as three, which you'll read). Perhaps you'll read

---

17. Israel Regardie, *The Golden Dawn* (St. Paul, MN: Llewellyn, 1989).

most of the cards in the stack; perhaps you'll read only a couple. Either is fine; it just means more or less is going on.[18]

8. You probably won't read every card, so what about the ones you don't read? They're not irrelevant: they offer some detail about the cards they are adjacent to. You can fine-tune meaning, and determine if a card is benevolent or malevolent, by the cards that flank it.

This is a difficult procedure to explain in the abstract, so let's give a specific example. Once you see it play out, you'll see how easy it is, and also how useful it can be. (And if you wish to read with the whole deck, you can modify this spread for the whole deck by counting the number of pips. Count aces as five. Queens, kings, and knights are four. Pages are seven. You may wish to extend the row to ten cards, if you do this.)

Count as Three	0–The Fool, XII–The Hanged Man, XX–Judgement
Count as Seven	I–The Magician, II–The High Priestess, III–The Empress, X–The Wheel of Fortune, XVI–The Tower, XIX–The Sun, XXI–The World
Count as Twelve	IV–The Emperor, V–The Hierophant, VI–The Lovers, VII–The Chariot, VIII–Strength, IX–The Hermit, XI–Justice, XIII–Death, XIV–Temperance, XV–The Devil, XVII–The Star, XVIII–The Moon

For my example reading, let's imagine I've just made an error in my investments that has lost me some money. I need to know how to proceed. So I shuffle the cards and ask, "What do I need to know about the past, present, and future of my financial situation?" I lay them out in the following tableau:

---

18. Mathematically astute readers will notice that counting twelve is equivalent, in a row of seven, of counting five. And counting seven will always land you on the previous card. However, since this same method can be used with other, larger tableaux, I'm offering the original numbers in the table. Feel free to take shortcuts.

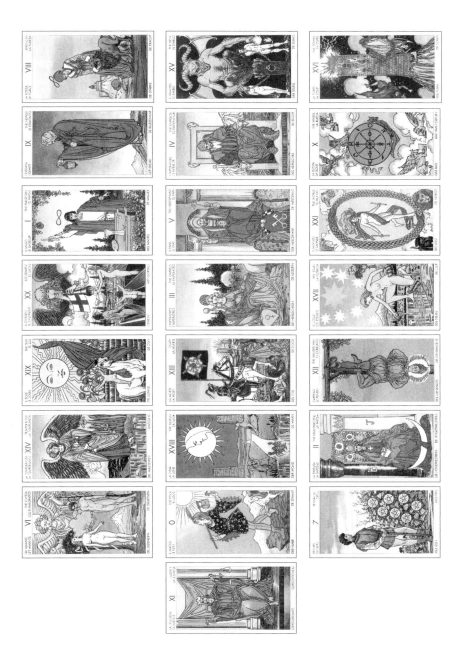

Justice as the overall theme card is reassuring to some degree. The loss isn't large and can be made up, apparently, making me break even.

Some choices [Lovers] have proven foolish [Fool] but there's a way out [Chariot] that will allow me to break even [Justice].

I would read the past line as follows.

The Lovers (count 12 to ...)	Some choices I have made ...
The Magician (count 7 to ...)	... involving education ...
Judgement (count 3 to ...)	... and a change in lifestyle ... (viz., I was in college a very, very long time)
The Hermit (count 12 to ...)	... and a career in teaching and writing ...
The Sun (count 7 to ...)	... have proven beneficial ...
Temperance (count 12 to ...)	... and wisely balanced.
The Hermit, so since this is a repeat, we stop.	

Wow, that's a lot of cards. I've had an eventful financial past, but since I had to be in college so long, I often wondered if the poverty and the loans would prove worth it. This tableau reminds me that, in fact, it has been. I've made good financial decisions in the past: I must not forget that just because one investment turned out unwise. This helps put it all into perspective.

In the present, my theme card is the Fool, which describes me fairly well, in both its negative and positive aspects.

The Fool (count 3 to ...)	Jumping in without double-checking ...
Death (count 12 to ...)	... has led to a loss due to confusion (the adjacent Moon card indicates this).
The Devil (count 12 to ...)	There's no way out of this mistake ...
The Empress (count 7 to ...)	... but overall, there's still growth. Don't panic (from the adjacent Hierophant).
Death, again, so since that's a repeat, we stop.	

And that's pretty accurate. A mistake led to a loss of funds that wasn't reversible. But it was a small amount of money, relative to my other investments. And so maybe, through growth, there's a way to recoup that money. Growth of money is interest. Hm.

In the future, my theme card is the Chariot. That means overcoming difficulties, but it also reminds me of my car, on which I owe a certain sum.

The Chariot (count 12 to ...)	My car ...
The World (count 7 to ...)	... can be brought full circle ...
The Star (count 12 to ...)	... and offer some freedom and hope.
The Chariot, which is a repeat, so we stop.	

That seems a bit opaque, unless the Chariot doesn't mean my car. But my intuition is that it does. What does the sense of completion offered by the World indicate in the financial world? Paying off a loan, perhaps. The Wheel of Fortune, adjacent to the World, reminds me of the principle of cumulative interest. And the Hanged Man is adjacent to the Star: that's one bill I can hang to dry, as it were. I look at what I owe on my car, calculate the amortization, and realize that if I used some of my savings to pay off my car, I would save almost as much money in interest as I lost previously. After a few more calculations, I get online and do just that. Now I've not only avoided that interest, I've given myself an effective raise every month.

Wow, ain't divination dandy.

Okay, most people probably don't need divination to make financial decisions, and the notion of using my savings to pay off my car early had occurred to me before. But the divination pointed out that it was a good idea and that I should pursue it. And best of all, it got me off my butt.

By the way, some time later I received a check from the financing company informing me of an error in my favor. I had overpaid and they were sending me a reimbursement. It was $50 shy of the original lost amount.

Let's try another one, this time rethinking the three levels as plot, characters, and setting of a particular "story." Let's imagine we have a querent who comes to us asking about an upcoming business trip. He's to present some fairly iconoclastic information to a group of experts, and he is a bit nervous that they might be a touch hostile.

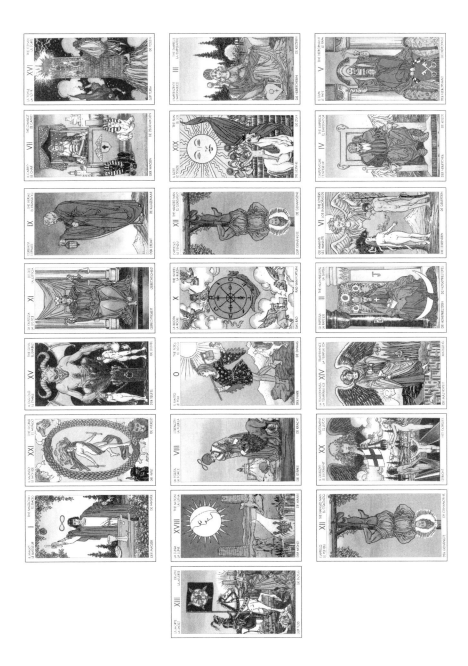

Card XIII, Death, is the theme card. This conference represents a change. If we were reading with the minor arcana, we might say "a big change," but instead this could just be something new: perhaps even just the first time the querent has been to this particular city—which it is.

Still using the counting method described above, we read the first line as "plot." The plot tells us that the querent's skills (the Magician) will be tested (the Tower) but will overcome (the Chariot) constraints (the Devil).

"What kind of restraints?" our querent asks.

We look to the cards flanking the Devil, as well as those below it. "Your ideas will be weighed (Justice) against common knowledge (the World), and many people will simply lack the insight to understand them (the Fool)."

The characters in this little drama are revealed in the middle line. Still counting, we have here dreamy (the Moon) and idealistic (the Star) people, who are nevertheless capable, intelligent (Strength), and bright (the Sun).

The setting is the Hanged Man, indicating that there won't be much traveling around once there. This card could presage a trip that involves a lot of time just hanging around the hotel room. "I kind of loathe the social parts of these things. Too much drinking, too much posturing," the querent says.

"Well, good news: you won't be doing much drinking or be around people who are (Temperance). But there will be an atmosphere of high expectation and traditions (the Hierophant), especially of your superiors (the Emperor is adjacent to the Hierophant); this is an environment that calls for wisdom (the High Priestess)." Of course, as it is an academic conference, this rings true.

One point of these examples is that the meaning of the cards exists only in relationship, either to the situation or to each other. In questions about a trip, the Hanged Man might indicate delays or "hanging out," while in questions about spirituality, it might indicate a personal sacrifice. Similarly, next to the Hierophant, the Hanged Man will take on qualities of sacrifice and initiation; next to the Lovers, it'll be a deferred choice; next to the Emperor, it might indicate "being hung out to dry" by the powers that be.

A similar relationship between the cards and their context exists in the Lenormand, and most Lenormand spreads are designed to capitalize on the power of these combinations. Many spreads are somewhat similar to the tarot tableaux I describe above, which is why I wanted to introduce it to those unfamiliar with this way of reading the tarot. In the next chapter, we'll take a look at some traditional and newer ways of reading the Lenormand.

CHAPTER IX

Some Lenormand Spreads

Your first impulse in picking up a Lenormand deck might be to read it just like the tarot, assigning positions and laying out cards. That's not necessarily a bad instinct. Any perusal of the few books in English on Lenormand will give you a few such spreads. In that sense, we can say that we read the Lenormand the same way we read the tarot.

But there are some differences, and they have to do with the structure of the symbols. As we've seen, the Lenormand symbols represent day-to-day occurrences, especially in the life of an eighteenth-century bourgeois woman, with a pronounced Romantic bent. Our experiences and concerns are closer to the bourgeois of the eighteenth century than they are to the monks of the Middle Ages or the scholars of the eighteenth century, which might be one reason that the Lenormand feels so "practical."

Let's explore some of the differences in the structure of the Lenormand with an eye toward how they will help us develop Lenormand spreads, including the Book of Life and Sylvie Steinbach's No Layout spread.

Situation Cards

Situation cards are sometimes called "signifiers," and there are a lot more of them in the Lenormand than in the tarot. Nearly any card could become a signifier for a question, but in practice there are a few cards that most readers use, again and again.

Two cards, 28–Gentleman and 29–Lady, are the most important signifiers. They signify a man and his wife, or a woman and her husband. If your querent is a man, he is 28–Gentleman and his wife or girlfriend is 29–Lady. If a woman, 29–Lady is the signifier, and 28–Gentleman is her husband or boyfriend. Everything here breaks down nicely by gender.

If you happen to be gay, or reading for a gay querent, then you need a third card, which is 18–Dog. That might seem insulting, but the Dog represents a close friend of either gender, and so is an all-purpose card for someone you know well. You could also—and perhaps more often will—use this card to indicate a friend, romantically or not. I've also noticed that, at least for me, the card of opposite gender sometimes just means "partner," regardless of sex or gender.

Cards can also represent issues. For example, if you want to know about someone's health, 5–Tree will tell you what you wish to know (need I mention the importance of going to a doctor, as well as consulting the cards, and not using the cards as substitutes for medical advice from a qualified professional? If so, consider it mentioned). If your querent is curious about money, you might use 34–Fish or 15–Bear, with 34–Fish representing independent wealth and investments, while 15–Bear indicates individual cash flow and personal wealth. Stock dividends are 34–Fish, while your paycheck from work is 15–Bear. And if there's a question about work, some traditional Lenormand readers would have you use 35–Anchor, while many American Lenormand readers (including me) prefer 14–Fox as a signifier of one's job.

In theory, any Lenormand card can represent the issue with which it is connected. A question about whether or not a letter will arrive, a book will be published, or for that matter a tower be built could all easily be associated with a card. In practice, a few cards come up again and again. For common signifiers, see the table below, which offers suggestions for possible signifiers.

Table of Possible Signifiers

Question	Possible Signifier
Money	15–Bear
Family; real estate	4–House
Love	24–Heart
Partnership; contracts	25–Ring
A friend or lover	29–Lady;
	28–Gentleman;
	18–Dog
Work	14–Fox
Health	5–Tree
A trip	3–Ship

You can choose to make a card the signifier in a given reading by deliberately associating it with the issue it is to signify. In most readings, you'll at least want to do this with 28–Gentleman or 29–Lady, to associate it with the querent.

You can create this association by pulling the card and holding it, while looking at the querent. Mentally imagine the querent's features transferring to the card, and when you feel this process is complete, reshuffle. If the querent isn't present, you can call the card by the querent's name: "You are so and so" a few times, then shuffle it back into the deck. If you're reading for yourself, you might find it useful to imagine yourself in the card, looking through the eyes of the person pictured. I might visualize myself striding in the garden, wearing a top hat and reading a letter (I look excellent in a top hat). Then add the card back to the deck and reshuffle.

For signifiers of issues, you need to imagine the object or idea associated with the card. The process is much the same: if I want to know what'll happen with my family as a whole, I imagine my house and household taking the place of the house in 4–House. If I'm asking about work, I might imagine the fox in 14–Fox sitting under my desk instead of under a bush.

This can be done quickly, and once you become familiar with the cards, you won't need to take them from the deck to do it: you can just visualize them from memory.

Book of Life or Grand Tableau

Once you link one or more cards with an issue, you can use the traditional spread called the Book of Life, also known as the Grand Tableau, to answer a number of questions at once. This Book of Life spread actually gives a snapshot of the month or so to come, in my experience, although you can fine-tune it by asking it to give a longer or shorter period of time. You could even do a Book of Life spread for the next day or so, although that would probably be so much more detail than you would ever need.

There are as many ways to read the Book of Life as there are Lenormand readers. Different readers even have different ways of laying out the tableau. The most common way I see is to lay out four rows of eight, with a row of four below them and centered. But Juan García Ferrer suggests laying the cards out in four rows of nine.[19] He offers an extremely complete and complex description of all of the ways of reading the cards in the Book of Life spread.

In general, techniques for reading these cards can be broken into two rough categories: common techniques and uncommon techniques. Readers differ on how they do everything from laying out the cards to determining the lines of present and future. But they do agree on some basic principles. The system I lay out here is my own homebrew, built out of those common techniques and what works for me. If you're interested in learning some other, more advanced techniques, you can do a lot worse than Ferrer's *El Método Lenor-*

---

19. Juan García Ferrer, *El Método Lenormand: Todo Sobre las Cartas Lenormand* (n. l. self-published, 2008).

mand, although as far as I know there is not an English edition. You will eventually need to invent your own method, just as I have, and it will appear as strange to other Lenormand readers as this description might appear to those who learned a different tradition. Just as we each develop a unique way of speaking, we each develop a unique way of interacting with the Lenormand's symbols.

Step 1. Before laying out the cards, identify one or more signifiers through the process outlined above.

Step 2. Then shuffle the cards according to your preferred ritual. At this point, authors disagree. Some deal from the bottom of the deck, some the top; some fan the cards out. Do what you prefer and whatever feels most natural. I just deal from the top of the deck, as if laying out a game of solitaire.

Step 3. Lay out the cards in four rows of eight with a row of four centered below.

Step 4. Read the first card. This is a general theme of the reading. Imagine that its meaning is a sort of diffuse light over which everything else can be seen. Don't make the overstatement mistake. If it's card 25–Ring, don't jump to the conclusion that the querent will be married. Instead, realize that promises, contracts, and groups of people might all be important during the time of the reading.

Step 5. Find the querent's signifier. If the signifier is to the far right, that means the future might be somewhat unclear. If to the far left, then the past might be unclear, or this might be the start of a brand-new phase of life, one without much of a past. If near the top, the querent might be just coasting through life during this period; if at the bottom, the querent may be overwhelmed with plans and ideas.

Step 6. Read the cards to the right, top, left, and bottom of the querent. These cards describe the querent's current condition.

Step 7. Read the cards above the querent in a line going up. These reflect things just coming into being, plans and ideas.

Step 8. Read the cards below the querent in a line going down. These reflect things the querent is overcoming or repressing.

Step 9. Read the cards in front of the querent stretching to the right (or, in some systems, in the direction the figure in the card is facing—whichever works for you). These reflect the possible futures.

Step 10. Read the cards behind the querent, stretching to the left. These reflect the past.

Step 11. Read the diagonals.

The upward-right diagonal reflects plans about the future.

The downward-right diagonal reflects unknown, unconscious, or unrecognized future possibilities.

The diagonal upward-left reflects past ideas and plans.

The diagonal downward-left reflects obstacles overcome or memories forgotten.

When reading the lines, it's important to "chunk" cards into combinations of two or three, in order to create a smooth narrative. There are pages and pages of combinations listed in various books, but really you need to construct them yourself. This issue of combinations gets into the grammar of the symbols of these cards, which I'll go into later in greater depth, but in general ask yourself, "What cards seem to go together?" The first card is the topic, the next card or two the comment. So if 25–Ring comes up, you might say the topic is promises. What kind of promises? If 18–Dog follows it, friendly ones. That naturally leads to "what about?" which should be answered by the next card: say it's 13–Child, then perhaps they're promises to babysit or watch someone's children. But what if it's 19–Tower? Ring followed by Tower would mean legal promises, but what if the Dog's in between? Then perhaps it means a friendly promise from someone in authority, maybe a lawyer, who is a sort of legal friend, or perhaps you should start a new combination with Tower asking, "Okay, a kind of power or authority—what kind?" and look to the next card. If it's 6–Clouds, it's a confusing kind. So you could read 25–Ring, 18–Dog, 19–Tower, and 6–Clouds as a promise from a friend involving a confusing authority: oh, it's a friend's promise to help you with your taxes! Over all, rely on your personal intuition, keeping in mind the role of the individual imagination in the philosophy of this deck's designers.

This procedure constitutes the basic method of gaining the general gist. There are several ways to proceed from here.

After reading the personal signifier, you may wish to find other signifiers. For example, the querent might say, "How will my job go this month?" You could look, depending on your system, for 14–Fox or 35–Anchor to answer that question. I prefer using 14–Fox for work, so I would use that. Then read it just like the personal signifier above. If one of the lines from a signifier intersects with the personal signifier card, that signifier's influence will be felt. Distance also matters: those things more distant from the signifier are less, well, significant. Some traditional readers read signifiers close to the personal signifier as more negative than those away: for example, 5–Tree near a signifier might indicate, some traditions say, a health problem, while far away it would mean a clean bill of health. I don't like that method at all. 5–Tree near the signifier just means the signifier is thinking about or will be involved in his or her health. It could just as easily, depending on surrounding cards, indicate a healthier lifestyle. Although in some cases, such as 15–Bear, which often represents money and cash flow, the distance between the card and the signifier is relevant. If 15–Bear is far away from the signifier, it might mean that cash flow is distant—either the querent isn't concerned about it, or someone else handles it, or there is none. Other cards around 15–Bear will explain which. So distance does matter, but it's not always knee-jerk negative or positive. It depends on logic, common sense, and intuition.

Once you finish hunting down signifiers and so forth, you may be stuck on a few cards. Perhaps you're not sure and want some more insight on individual signifiers. Fortunately, a more advanced technique, the technique of houses, lets you do that.

Each of the positions, starting from one to thirty-six, has an "invisible" card on it, associated with the number of its position. So, for example, if the signifier 28–Gentleman lands on the fifteenth place, you can imagine a ghost card of 15–Bear with it. These invisible cards, the houses, offer an "in other words" reading. If 28–Gentleman lands on 15–Bear, I might say, "You've got some cash flow issues." Whether good or bad should be readable from the other cards. I can also use this to help describe a person: if 18–Dog lands on the twenty-third place, I can say, "This is your friend, the kind of squirrelly, mousy one who's always mooching off of you," because 18–Dog takes on some of the characteristics of 23–Mouse from its location.

The technique of houses is useful in identifying people; however, you can get even more detail if you look at the cards on the corners of any card you suspect of representing a person. So if you're reading the future, and you have the friend who's going to help you with your taxes, a querent might say, "Wait, which friend?" You can look, first, at the house, but you can also check out the corner cards of 18–Dog to refine the meaning. Say you have 1–Rider, 13–Child, 29–Lady, and 22–Crossroad. From this, I know that the person is athletic, kind of childish—or maybe a new friend who has just come into the querent's life—feminine, and perhaps a bit indecisive. Some cards lend themselves better to description than others; don't be afraid to say, "I don't know what that card means there" if something doesn't fit.

The technique of houses, by the way, explains why we read the first card as a general indicator of the spread. The first house is 1–Rider, which represents a visitor or a message. And what's the most current, relevant message occurring in this particular moment? The one the reader is offering the querent, presumably.

All six cards in the corners of the tableau, because of the houses they occupy, indicate general trends about the reading. It can be important to read these cards; they can cast a light on the rest of the spread. The first card, as we said, is the general trend of the reading:

you can think of it as what's coming in. The last card of the first line, card number 8, is what's ending or going out, because it is associated with 8–Coffin, which represents endings. The card in the left-hand bottom corner, card number 25, indicates the role of partners or others around the person, because 25–Ring represents the promises of others. The card at the end of that last long line, card number 32, tells us the emotional state of the querent, because that is one of the roles of 32–Moon. The next card, 33, tells us the nature of any recent key events, as it is associated with 33–Key. It might identify those events, or just tell us about them. Finally, the last card, 36, is often the place of worries or fears about the future, or spiritual matters if relevant to the querent and question, because its house is 36–Cross.

Following is an actual example I did for a stranger online, which isn't optimal, of course, as I prefer face-to-face, where the querent can offer context and answer questions. But this example will illustrate a few important points, as well as how a reader can make a preconception that causes him (me, that is) to miss something important.

A querent comes asking for a reading. She says she prefers to get a general forecast, and only then ask questions. While it's usually nice if a querent comes with questions, you can really go out on a limb this way and be brave. I'll give my actual reading, mistakes and all, so you can see how a reading develops and how a good reading involves some give and take with the querent. Again, this isn't cold reading: when I'm wrong, I admit it.

I lay out the tableau as follows:

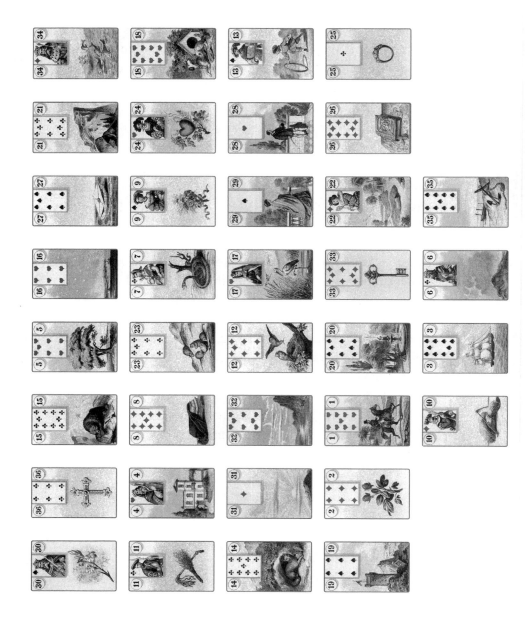

30–Lily is a nice card to start with: it tells me that everything will work out fine.

I find the signifier, 29–Lady. I look first to her past, which is long. She's had a life-changing event recently (17–Stork). What kind of event? A conversation (12–Birds) about feelings and dreams (32–Moon). She also had a bit of happiness involving her job: a dream job, as it were. In her future is a man (28–Gentleman) and a child (13–Child) or perhaps a childish man, or a new start with a man. Above her, it seems she trying to find some beautiful words (9–Flowers, 27–Letter). Below her, she has put off making a choice (22–Crossroad) about her lifestyle (35–Anchor). She dreams of being adventurous in love (24–Heart, 34–Fish), and has perhaps put off school (26–Book) for this man. In the past, she's been ill (5–Tree, 7–Snake). I suspect, because of 15–Bear, this illness may have involved food in some way, and 16–Star means it might be psychological. She may also have taken an important trip recently (3–Ship, 33–Key).

Let's look at this man. He has a mountain on his heart: he has a hard time expressing his emotions. He's also suppressing secrets (26–Book). In the past, his path has been cloudy: he has had a hard time making an important decision. But let's look at his corners: 18–Dog indicates that he's known to this woman already, and 9–Flowers tells me that he's attractive. 22–Crossroad tells me that he keeps his options open, but 25–Ring tells me he might be willing to commit. And 25–Ring is also in his future, in the deferred or avoided future. But I'm going out on a limb: he's proposed and they're getting married. As you'll see, this limb will crack under my weight later, because I did not attend to the place of 25–Ring closely enough.

It's always worthwhile to take a look at the place of 15–Bear in the tableau, as it can indicate ready cash. It's rather far from the Lady card, which usually means some cash flow problems. 36–Cross speaks of worries in the past, which have turned out just fine (30–Lily). Below the Bear is 8–Coffin and 32–Moon: the worries about money have led to feeling as if all dreams have to be boxed up and set away. There's a dread of painful news (1–Rider, 10–Scythe). In the future, though, we see reliance on family (5–Tree) and hope (16–Star), but the bills (27–Letters) pile up (21–Mountains). Eventually, though, there's a good omen: 34–Fish speaks of financial independence.

At this point, I ask the querent what she thinks. First, she tells me I've got it all wrong: for one thing, she's gay. This tendency toward heterosexism and sexism is a drawback of the Lenormand. I tend to read the Gentleman and Lady cards as more general "people" cards, often of any gender, but here I jumped to a conclusion you'd think I would have avoided, being gay myself. And, she says, my limb is cracking, because in fact she has recently proposed and her partner has said no and moved out! Obviously, in retrospect, she "turns down" the ring, because 25–Ring is in the lower diagonal. She's not sure, she says, how she'll survive on just her income, which is moderate. She may have to leave her house (4–House, 8-Coffin).

If I had read the corners more closely, I might have realized a lot of this. What's ending is her independence (34–Fish). Although I took that to mean that she would be getting married, it was much more financially literal than I suspected. Card 19–Tower can indicate isolation, which is in the place of her partner, and what's affecting her emotions is 25–Ring, the proposal. The key event is clear: 10–Scythe, which traditionally has almost always meant a breakup. And finally, her fears are represented by 35–Anchor: she fears that she will not be able to maintain her lifestyle.

Yet I stand by this: Lily is in the first place, and I still see the two of them together, in a new (13–Child) relationship (or, perhaps, literally with a child!). It's clear now to me that the beautiful thing she wishes to craft out of words is a way of winning her partner back. Will it work? It's hard to see for sure, but the partner is still in the querent's future, at least as a friend, perhaps as more. They do share fond emotions (24–Heart).

Fortunately, other factors, including the fact that she does enjoy her job, despite its moderate income and her past dealing with a food-related disorder, were accurate and helpful insights for the querent. The error on my part was in jumping to conclusions and reading into the tableau what I wanted to see. This is an instructive error, because it's very easy to fall into it, particularly when the querent is absent and you want to be nice.

This reading illustrates one of the drawbacks of the Grand Tableau or Book of Life spread: it can make fiddly distinctions of great importance. The place where the Ring lands around the Gentleman card affects its meaning. Yet if 18–Dog had landed there, would that have made him (in this case, I suppose, her) less friendly? No, it's a matter of context, and it's difficult to define hard and fast rules.

And the querent's role in determining that context is important. If I say, "This is a man who ... " and the querent says, "Are you sure it's not a woman?" it may well be. As a reader, you need to rely not just on the cards and their meanings, but the context provided by the querent and no less importantly your own intuition.

The other drawback of the Book of Life is that it takes a long time. Sometimes, you have a simple question and want to know the answer immediately. There are two other spreads you can use when you wish to answer this kind of question, which I imagine will be the most common spreads used by most readers. I use one of these two methods more often than I use the Grand Tableau. Both of them, however, rely on the same skills as the Book of Life: perception of patterns, parsing and reading a line of cards, and understanding cards by their positions.

Sylvie Steinbach describes a unique system she calls the "no layout" spread.[20] I do not wish to step on her toes: my brief explanation cannot substitute for reading her book. In essence, she charges one or more signifiers, then draws cards until that signifier appears. She reads two or three cards on either side of that signifier to get information about the near past and future of the querent. She explains that one can charge multiple signifiers in a single reading: 29–Lady, for the querent; 4–House for her family; 15–Bear for her cash flow situation. This method is, if you think about it, essentially an abbreviated Book

---

20. Sylvie Steinbach, *The Secrets of the Lenormand Oracle* (Lexington, KY: BookSurge Publishing, 2007).

of Life: instead of laying out the whole tableau, one just lays out the near future and past of the relevant signifiers.

This signifier becomes the theme upon which the other cards act as elaboration. This process is similar to that of the tarot, in which we say, "This card, the Knight of Wands, represents you," or "This place is the place of the future." Note that in the tarot, we can charge a card as signifier, or we can charge a location in the spread with meaning. Both methods are similar. We simply project that meaning, either upon the card's image in our imagination, or upon the location on the table where we intend to set the card. Similarly, we can charge locations on the table , just as we can charge cards in the Lenormand with meaning.

A similar spread to the No Layout spread, and one that I'll explain in greater depth, does much the same. But in this case, you do not charge a signifier but a location on the table. You still charge it as a card, however. So, for example, you might decide to charge a location with the querent's identity: 28–Gentleman, let's say. Now I lay five cards, with the middle card on the place I have charged as 28–Gentleman. Now we read that card as if it is in combination with the querent: it expresses his current state. The cards on either side are read as past and future trends.

We can again charge multiple signifiers and do what I'll call the Petit Tableau. The Petit Tableau can answer a more specific question than the Grand Tableau and takes less time. Essentially, we charge two locations on the table: one for the querent, by visualizing the appropriate cards (usually 28–Gentleman or 29–Lady) projected or visualized in that place; and one for the question, by projecting or visualizing the appropriate signifier card on the place below it. For example, if the querent is asking about money, we might project 15–Bear. If about love, 24–Heart. If about partnership, 25–Ring.

These charged locations then become the "houses" of those concerns. We can do any number of these; but I recommend starting with just two at a time, one house for the querent and one for the question.

Now, lay out five cards on each row, so that the middle card lands on the charged house. In the horizontal rows, read the cards in front as future; those behind as past. So you'll have the theme cards, landing on the houses, related to the cards those houses are charged to. You'll also have the future of the querent, the past of the querent, the future of the question, and the past of the question. You can also read how these trends interact by looking at the combinations created by the cards that land above each other in the spread.

Let me give you a quick example. Imagine that a querent comes to you asking about his job. How are things going at work? What will happen in the near future? The querent is a man, so we charge for 28–Gentleman, and work is the Fox, so we charge for 14–Fox (or maybe we'd prefer charging for 35–Anchor if we're using European traditional associations). I lay out the cards with the theme card first, then the other four cards on either side in an alternating pattern, like this:

4	2	1	3	5
9	7	6	8	10

Doing so, after shuffling thoroughly and performing our preferred starting ritual, we end up with:

Now, we read starting with the middle card of the top row, charged with signifier. This is saying, "You're a kind of messenger." It could also mean "you're on horseback, moving forward." That's good news. To the right we have the Anchor: the message you're bringing is one of stability in the face of complexity and deception (7–Snake). So your role at work is to cut through the BS. In the past, there was a big decision (33–Key, 22–Crossroad), and you chose the best option. (Key is almost always a good card—I only read it as a disastrously bad event if the other cards are slapping me to do so.)

Now, as to the job: this is your dream job (30–Lily). You're content here, and have accomplished a goal. 4–House might mean the coworkers are like a family. ("Actually, I just bought a house," the querent says. "And I was concerned that I might not be able to keep it if something happened at work.") Well, not to worry! Because there you are: the rider has come home at the end of the first row.

8–Coffin sometimes means endings, but really it's about transformations, much like card XIII–Death in the tarot. Here we have transformation and 15–Bear, often a card of cash flow. Now, this might mean "cash flow comes to an end" if it were around another ending card, like Scythe. But it's not: instead, it means "boxes of money." In other words, a transformation in your financial situation. ("This current job more than doubled my current salary," the querent says. "But I still don't know if I have enough money for necessities.")

15–Bear means "cash flow." 30–Lily can mean "satisfied, enough." So we can tell the querent that he needn't worry: he's got enough. There might be lean times and fat times, but overall he's got what he needs here.

Now, we can read from top to bottom; unlike the horizontal rows, these are not necessarily situated in time. I tend to read them as comments on the present or predictions about the future, depending on intuition or the querent's response. We start in the middle and read 1–Rider with 30–Lily. "Good news is coming: a major project is nearly done." 35–Anchor, 4–House: "You've got a stable and long-term position." 22–Crossroad, 15–Bear: "Lots of options for making money; work isn't your only income stream." 33–Key, 8–Coffin: "Big changes coming, although not a job loss because of 35–Anchor. Instead, you might find yourself moving up, changing titles." 7–Snake, 28–Gentleman: "You're a bit devious; that can serve you well, or it can serve you badly. But be aware that you don't want a reputation for dishonesty."

"Well," the querent says. "I'm not terribly devious. But the rest is true. I'm angling for a promotion soon, and I did just finish a pretty large project."

Ahh, 7–Snake is the Queen of Clubs, and thus can represent a person. "Do you work closely with a somewhat sly older woman?"

"Oh, yes, now that's true! We work together on several projects."

Now it might be a good time to look at some of the other possible people cards, such as 4–House, which can also be the King of Hearts: "There's also a man here, stable and solid."

"My boss, I suspect."

"Could be. Judging from his closeness to 28–Gentleman, one of your signifiers, he likes you. There's also an older man."

"Yes, but he's retiring soon."

Aha. "Is he in a position of authority over you?"

"Not specifically, but he is well-regarded by most of my coworkers."

"Coffin + Bear + Lily could indeed indicate his retirement, opening up a place (house) for you."

The querent looks thoughtful. "So can this card, the Queen of Diamonds, 22–Crossroad also mean a person?"

"Possibly, but not necessarily. She'd also probably be a bit older than you, since she touches 30–Lily."

"Everyone is older than me."

"And she opens up (33–Key) opportunities and choices (22–Crossroad) for you."

"I'm not sure who that is."

"Keep an eye out, then."

The querent later reported that he did in fact get the promotion, as predicted, and that the reading fit quite well. He still hadn't identified the older woman, however, which might mean that it did not represent a woman after all.

Readings tend to go better when the reader can talk directly to the querent. When the two are separated, even by telephone, it's sometimes hard to get the necessary context, as in the first Book of Life example above. However, even there, if I had read the cards more carefully the first time I would have seen what I had missed. The one bit of context I was missing was the querent's sexual orientation, but really the dynamics of the situation remain the same even without taking into account that element. And the character sketch I drew of the querent's partner (or ex-partner) was considered accurate, apart from sex.

I included both of these readings to illustrate that a true reader of the cards makes mistakes, needs feedback from the querent, and works with the querent to create meaning rather than impose it on a querent. Reading the cards—or any oracle—is a collaborative effort with the querent.

CHAPTER X

The Grammar of Symbols

All cartomantic systems propose to define the future—or at least, to describe human experience—by means of a set number of symbols. In the tarot, we have potentially seventy-eight, although in this book we're mostly using the twenty-two major arcana. In the Petit Lenormand, we have thirty-six. In other systems, we may have even fewer, although there are few cartomantic decks with fewer than thirty-two cards.

Each card, therefore, must be a slice of life. Whether that slice is a thick one or a thin one is a function of the number of cards in the deck, as well as the nature of its symbols. The tarot has some thin slices, at least in the minor arcana, but each slice is large enough to cover an equal range of experience, largely due to the structure of the deck as a matrix. For example, in the minor arcana, each human endeavor is classified in one of four domains: wands, cups, swords, and pentacles. Moreover, in each of these four domains, four people are defined: the elder male, the elder female, the younger male, the younger female. Finally, in each domain, "what can happen" is divided into ten slices, the ten pip cards.

In the Lenormand, the cake has not been cut so cleanly, and there is overlap and fuzziness. However, this overlap is not a flaw, but a feature. One can read the overlaps as if each combination of cards is a potential Venn diagram of experience. A Venn diagram is a graphic representation of interlocking sets in which some members of one group share characteristics from another group. We can imagine Venn diagrams that describe the relationships between individual cards as sets of meaning. For example, if 15–Bear and 34–Fish come together, we know that the issue is one of money, because of the possible sets of meaning in these two cards, they share the idea of "money." However, if 15–Bear and 5–Tree come together, it might instead be one of health and food. Bear can indicate both cash flow and "food flow," if I may coin a term. Tree can indicate both family and health. Together they share the domain of the body.

This grammar of combinations is also true in the tarot, but to a lesser degree. The lines between the slices are more defined, less ragged. This, also, isn't a flaw. Sometimes it's useful to have a clean box to put experience in.

Ultimately, both approaches are features, not bugs. When we need a clean set of cubbyholes, we have the tarot. When we want a wide-open desktop to spread our ideas on, we have the Lenormand.

It's worth mentioning again that the tarot was not always so tidy. The occult revival of which Waite was a part helped to define some of the clear demarcations between ideas. Waite, and those around him, were modernists: they believed firmly in the meaningfulness of symbols. And they came from an occult tradition of natural magic, which sought to categorize all experience into taxonomical structures. Our current taxonomy of animals and plants is a legacy of this approach to knowledge.

When Waite and his fellow occultists took up the tarot, the work of categorization of its symbols had already been begun by Levi. They merely refined and defined these meanings. Still, some of the ragged edges had to stick out. For example, the Six of Swords traditionally meant "travel by water," probably for no other reason than it was an idea that needed a place. Waite's meaning for the Six of Swords, in his Pictorial Guide, hints at his ambivalence:

> A ferryman carrying passengers in his punt to the further shore. The course is smooth, and seeing that the freight is light, it may be noted that the work is not beyond his strength. *Divinatory Meanings*: journey by water, route, way, envoy, commissionary, expedient. *Reversed*: Declaration, confession, publicity; one account says that it is a proposal of love.

He tries to move out from the specificity of "water" to the idea of "way." He also tries to fit in the "proposal of love," by simply relegating it to the anonymous "one account." What Waite was dealing with were a dozen different ways of slicing this cake, and none of them agreed. Waite's images (or, more accurately, Pamela Colman Smith's images) helped cement this particular way of dividing the cake, so much so that even those who read older tarot decks sometimes use the meanings depicted in the Rider-Waite.

There has been no similar effort to categorize the Lenormand. The Petit Lenormand was, by its nature, rather underneath Waite's notice. While he could shuffle off "proposal of love" into a corner of a reversed meaning of one card in his book on the tarot, how might he have dealt with 25–Ring?

With one exception, I can find little reference to Marie-Anne Lenormand by any of the luminaries of the late nineteenth- and early twentieth-century occult revival, despite the fact that her name remained, and remains, synonymous with fortune-telling in Germany and France. Eliphas Levi, however, does mention her, and manages to criticize her learning, her politics (Legitimists were a pro-royal political movement), and—elsewhere—even her appearance:

> Mlle. Lenormand, the most celebrated of our modern fortune-tellers, was unacquainted with the science of the Tarot. … She knew neither high Magic nor the

Kabalah, but her head was filled with ill-digested erudition, and she was intuitive by instinct, which deceived her rarely. The works she left behind her are Legitimist tomfoolery, ornamented with classical quotations; but her oracles, inspired by the presence and magnetism of those who consulted her, were often astounding.[21]

So we see that Levi considers the tarot a science, which is to say, an organized system of knowledge, and the Lenormand method of reading, if not the deck of cards that bears her name, are ill-organized, incomplete, and rely excessively upon those womanly traits of intuition and enthusiasm. On the same page, he accuses her of "mental rambling" and "extravagance of imagination," which replace the "natural affections of her sex." Then he mentions her lack of beauty. This is a vicious attack of misogyny, even for this time: what is it that drives Levi to such cruelty? Many of the traits he describes—imagination, organic rather than ordered discourse (or "rambling")—are also the elements of the Romantic movement. I will explore this idea more fully in chapter thirteen. Levi is not *just* being sexist here; he is also taking a philosophical stand against Romanticism in favor of his own occult Neoclassicism.

We who wish to increase our intuition, to encourage our enthusiasm, would hardly find that a ringing denunciation. And even Levi offers her some praise, through the opaque veils of his sexism and classism. Her erudition is "ill-digested," her works "tomfoolery." But he can't deny that she was rarely wrong in her divinations, as much as he seems to want to. So, finally, he calls her ugly.

At one point, at least, the Lenormand—or the philosophy it reflects—and the tarot were at odds, to the point where usually intelligent and witty scholars like Levi could be reduced to playground taunts. Can the two systems hold hands as friends now, and if so, how do these symbols interact? What is the difference between the tarot and the Lenormand in the ways in which the symbols can be read?

---

21. Eliphas Levi, *Transcendental Magic* (Boston, MA: Weiser, 1968), 349–350.

Symbolic Domains

The first and greatest of differences is this: in the tarot, especially in the minor arcana, the symbolic domains are fixed. There are four categories of experience: air, water, earth, and fire; swords, cups, pentacles, and wands; or mind, emotions, body, and action. All permutations of the symbols of the minor arcana interact in those four symbolic domains.

But in the Lenormand, the symbolic domains are determined by the question. This relationship with symbols and their domains mirrors what we experience in most of the rest of our lives. Perhaps this is why I have heard several readers of both systems say that the tarot is like talking to a philosopher, while the Lenormand is like talking to a friend. A philosopher categorizes; a friend speaks in the expectation you will understand the relevant domains.

A symbolic domain, as I'm using the term here, is simply a collection of symbols around a particular idea. If I am going to talk about music, the symbols "bass" and "tempo" and "treble" are part of the domain. Many symbols can stretch across domains: for example, the word "bass" in music is pronounced differently and means something different from the word "bass" in fishing. Perhaps a better example is the experience of many college freshmen, who suddenly take an introductory course in a new field: psychology, mathematics, or biology. They quickly find themselves perusing and memorizing lists of words they thought they knew: "affect" and "function" and "mantle." But in the symbolic domains of those fields, those words take on new meaning: affect becomes a noun meaning emotional reaction; a function is a kind of equation; a mantle is a part of a mollusc.

Similarly, we quickly realize that 25–Ring is not always marriage. We must step back and get a larger view of the meaning of the card in this context. For example, if someone is asking about a business, perhaps it shows up in the future. Do you predict a proposal? Or do you step back and say, "A marriage is a kind of contract; businesses have their own kinds of contracts." You're probably going to generalize, at least if you're wise.

Each of the Lenormand cards can do this: sometimes, 18–Dog means "a dog" in the literal sense; sometimes it means "a friend," sometime "a partner," and sometimes just the abstract idea of "loyalty." It always depends upon the context.

This is true, as well, of the major arcana of the tarot. Rarely will XIII–Death mean actual death. Instead, it usually means change. And in some contexts, it might not even be an earth-shattering kind of change. In some imaginable contexts, it might just mean a change of socks.

It is a useful exercise with both the Lenormand and the tarot to take each card and permute it through certain symbolic domains. What would this card mean if it were about a relationship? About a business? About an artistic project? About a job? And so on. I've explained this procedure earlier, but if you haven't done it, now would be a good time to start thinking about how the symbols of the cards change in different contexts.

For example, if we take III–The Empress, in a relationship she represents nurturing love. In a business? Growth of the business. In an artistic project? Emotion and, perhaps, sentimentality. For a job? One with room for advancement and growth. What about card 23–Mouse: In love? Nagging worry and perhaps jealousy. In a business? Loss, perhaps from theft or unforeseen overhead. In an artistic project? Lack of focus and busywork. For a job? Busyness, but perhaps with no ultimate benefit.

We can break these down to small domains, if we like. As described briefly in chapter 2, Ferrer offers an exercise where one imagines what kind of car, house, etc., each of the cards might indicate.[22] So, for example, 31–Sun might indicate a big, bright, impressive sports car and a warm inviting house with lots of windows. Similarly, with the tarot, IX–the Hermit might indicate a "private" car, perhaps with tinted windows. Or perhaps it's a "seeking" car, one used

---

22. Juan García Ferrer, *El Método Lenormand: Todo Sobre las Cartas Lenormand* (n.l. self-published, 2008), 42.

for surveillance. The house will be lonely and secluded and contemplative.

I am tempted to create a table of my own for you to memorize, but if I do, I'll be defeating the real purpose, which is to slice that pie for yourself. I would encourage you to do this now, if you haven't already, for each of the cards in the Lenormand or the major arcana. Ask yourself, if this card were X, what kind of X would it be?

Write down your answers in a notebook or on your computer, so you can review and revise them later. Doing this in your head is good, too, but you'll want a record later. Especially as some of them will be puzzlers that you'll have to leave blank for the time being. For each, ask yourself "what kind of...

Car

House

Person

Job or career

Monetary situation

Relationship

Pastime or hobby

...would this card be?"

You can create some of your own categories. For example, if this card were a kind of movie, what kind of movie would it be? Would 10–Scythe be a horror movie? 34–Fish, an adventure movie?

Eventually, you will come to a stage in understanding the cards where you can classify your daily experience by means of them. So, for example, with the tarot, you might encounter a problem at work and think, "The boss was really IX–Hermit today, trying to guide everyone all the time. I kind of wish he'd let me XVII–Star and do it my own way."

For me, and perhaps for you, this is an easier process to accomplish with the Petit Lenormand than with the tarot. It's easier to say, "The boss was trying to be a 22–Crossroad kind of guy, but he really ended up just being 6–Clouds." The reason why these day-to-day concerns are a bit easier to relate to the Lenormand than the tarot lies in the nature of their symbols, and the fuzzy relationships each has to its meaning.

The Symbolic Nimbus

It's easy to assume that each symbol—be it a word or a cultural symbol—connects to a single meaning, so many people conceive of a direct line between a symbol and its meaning. But we know that meaning is actually much more complex than that. A symbol corresponds not to a single thing, but to a fuzzy set of things. For example, the symbol "dog" (I'm just talking about the word here, not the card) can refer to an animal. But it also contains ideas like loyalty and friendliness. At the same time, it can be an insult, a symbol of persistence ("she dogged me for that report"). I can call the animal a dog, sure, but I can call a person a dog, a picture of a dog a dog, a statue a dog. I can't refer to, say, cheese as a dog. But I can refer to a frankfurter as a dog, so food is not completely excluded.

It's more accurate to think of a symbol, not as pointing to a thing, but as a location on a kind of map, from which its various meanings are other locations. A meaning closer to the center of this map is one more often associated with the symbol. With "dog," the "animal" meaning is close to the center. Ideas closer to the edge are ideas less often associated with it. But the edge itself is fuzzy; we could apply "dog" metaphorically to nearly any concept. For some it would be a stretch. But we could still do it and be understood.

Around each of the cards of your cartomancy deck, whether the tarot or the Petit Lenormand or a deck of playing cards, is a nimbus or cloud of meaning. This is why 25–Ring doesn't mean "marriage" in every situation. It can apply to many different situations. And 21–Mountain means "delay," but "delay" itself means any number of things, depending on your own location in the overlapping fuzzy sets of meaning. A delay on a trip is a delayed flight, perhaps, or a mix-up at the hotel. A delay when asking about pregnancy tells of a late birth. A delay might even be a good thing, depending on the question.

Our job in reading the cards isn't matching each card with a meaning in a book or in our rote memory. Our job is mapping the location of the querent amid the overlapping nimbuses of the cards themselves.

This job is complicated by the relationship of a single card to several different fuzzy sets of meaning. The tarot, particularly, covers huge ground with each of the cards in the major arcana. But even the Lenormand displays a wide range of meanings. If we say that 21–Mountain means delay, it also means obstacles of all other varieties. And at the same time, it's a mountain and sometimes just means "mountain."

Traditional ways of reading the Lenormand have taken into account this structure of meaning, which is interesting when you realize the cards were made by the philosophically naïve in a time when no one, not even philosophers, understood meaning this way. Perhaps the creators of these cards were not so naïve as we thought.

Combinations

In the Lenormand, combinations of cards take on more detailed and nuanced meanings than cards alone. I've already described this in brief, but there's more to the grammar of these combinations than has been described above.

The structure of any Lenormand combination is what we call in linguistics a topic-comment structure. The *topic* is what we're talking about. The *comment* is what is said about that topic. So, in the simplest form, we can think of the topic as the subject and the comment as the predicate of a sentence: "Bill eats cake." Bill is the topic. His eating of cake is the comment on Bill. But it can become rather more complex in language; we can reverse the order of these things. "Cake is what Bill ate." In this case, by placing "cake" first, we've made it the topic, and Bill's eating becomes the comment.

There are two ways of creating the topic-comment distinction in cartomancy. The first is that the location in the spread determines the topic, and the card that lands upon it is the comment. So if I lay VIII–Strength in the place of "hopes," the topic is "hope" and the comment is the complex, fuzzy set of meanings attached to VIII–Strength. I discard some of those meanings because they do not fit with the topic, and others because they do not match the context, and then select one that fits my felt sense.

We can also read combinations of tarot cards, making one card the topic and the other the comment. Lay down two cards, one after the other. The first is the topic; the next is the comment. So I lay down X–Wheel of Fortune, and say to the querent, "There has been an upset in your fortunes, perhaps a turn for the positive." I turn over the next card and say, "This is Strength. It shows that change in your fortune has given you increased power and responsibility." The Wheel of Fortune is the topic: a change in fortune. The Strength card defines the results of that change of fortune. This is what we do with the three-card reading, in which the middle card takes on the topic and the other two cards provide comment on that theme.

In the Lenormand, similarly, we can read two cards in sequence as a topic and comment. But we can also charge a place. As already explained, one common reading method is to project the signifier card on the middle place of three or five cards. One then reads the signifier as the topic, and the card that lands on that place as the comment.

The other complexity is that a comment can become a new topic with its own comment. So, "Bill eats cake. The cake was delicious." In one sentence, the comment is "eats cake." In the next, this comment is picked up and transformed into a topic. Similarly, once I read the projected signifier as the topic, and the card that lands on that place as the comment, I can combine those two meanings and use them as a topic that the other cards act as another comment for.

These interactions can become extremely complicated. Some books on the Lenormand offer lists of combinations, but I find them of relatively little use. Instead, it's better to understand how the topic and comment of combinations fit together in cartomancy. At least, if you have a mind like I do, it's better. I like to reason things out for myself.

There are multiple ways a topic and a comment can relate in cartomancy. Below I will explain some, and then give a concrete example of how they might be used in a reading.

1. Equation (T = C). The comment may be equated with the topic, as in "Pizza is what I want for supper." In this case, the topic of pizza equates to the comment of "what I want for supper." Similarly, two cards can lie in a combination that encourages equation of their two symbols. If I have 27–Letter and 25–Ring, I can see the topic, the documents, equated with the ring, a promise: this is a combination that can indicate a contract, in which the document *is* a promise.

2. Description (T is like C). Closely related to equation are combinations of description. In "This pizza is good," the topic of the pizza has the comment of goodness. Similarly, 28–Gentleman and 23–Mice might indicate a person (the topic) who is mousey (the comment). This combination blends into the next, as well, which is:

3. Classification (C is a type of T). In this combination, the comment is a kind of thing or a subset of things identified by the topic. So 36–Cross as the topic, and 11–Whip as the comment, might indicate a kind of pain or burden that is physical or sexual in nature. As you can see, this relationship is much like that of description above.

4. Action (T does C). The above three combinations are those that many readers rely upon, but it's important to remember that each of the cards is also an action, as well as an object. Here, we can see the comment acting as a verb or active predicate. So

15–Bear followed by 7–Snake could be a powerful person like a boss who betrays someone.

These four relationships are marked in language through choices in syntax and grammar. But in the Lenormand or tarot, all we have are two cards lying next to each other. How, then, can we know which relationship applies? Moreover, how can we know which of several possible meanings for each card apply?

The answer, simply put, is intuition: which is an answer that answers nothing. However, in the next chapter, I will describe specific techniques you can employ to use your intuition as a specific tool to help discern what the cards mean in any given pattern.

CHAPTER XI

Intuitive Reading

Here's the bit of the book where I launch into the woo-woo. I obviously don't think it's woo-woo; on the contrary, while I'm a staunch advocate for rational thinking (there's too little of it; too few people know how to do it; and those who claim it rarely practice it), I also think there's a place for the nonrational. Note that the nonrational isn't the irrational. Rather than the opposite of rational thinking, it's the complement to it.

We can divide rational thinking into two ways of reasoning: deduction and induction. Similarly, we can identify nonrational thinking as comprised of a third: abduction. Deductive reasoning is mathematical in nature: it arrives at a conclusion that necessarily follows from given premises. Induction is scientific: it arrives at conclusions based upon weighing evidence. Both involve analysis, the process of breaking ideas into their parts. Abduction, in contrast, is the perception of patterns and the creation of meaning from those patterns holistically. Where both deduction and induction analyze patterns into their components, when we use abduction we perceive the patterns as a whole.

When we read the cards, we don't abandon analysis: we analyze the cards and their places to narrow down a range of possible meanings. For some readers, this analysis is all they do: the beginner frantically flipping through the book and reading the "meanings" of the cards is performing a kind of analysis. It has value, to be sure, or no beginner would ever move beyond those beginnings.

However, skilled readers shoud use abduction, too. Abduction isn't a mystical process; nearly every scientist begins with an abduction. Let's imagine that I'm investigating a scientific problem. I notice that the current theories of, say, syntax don't quite work for me. I can't put my finger on it, but I have a hunch that it works some other way. This hunch, which leads to potential hypotheses, is abductive reasoning. I have seen the pattern and "felt" that it doesn't fit. Now, as a scientist, I design procedures by which I can try to falsify my hunch, leading me into the city streets of induction and deduction.

But let's imagine that we remain in the twisty forest path of abductive reasoning for a while longer. Scientists use this tool only to find things to investigate, but can we use it as a means of investigation itself? Can we use it to create meaning?

Poets and artists use abductive reasoning all the time. A poem begins—at least for me—in a felt sense of rightness about a phrase or a few words. I might have two phrases, know that they must be separated, that I must move from one to the other, but know nothing else. Then, word by word, phrase by phrase, on a good day clause by clause, I find the rest of the poem.

So how do we use abduction? What is the procedure?

I've already discussed focusing, and suggested that this method could be used to derive at more effective questions. It can also help us understand meanings. We can "hold" a possible meaning in our body, and wait for a response. So, for example, I have the combination of 17–Stork and 9–Flowers. I understand the stork is the theme of change and improvement, and the flowers indicate beauty or a gift. So this is an improvement in beauty. I relax and pay attention to my body. Where do I wish to hold this idea?

I feel my attention drift, let's say, to my belly (although it could just as easily be any other part of the body—and sometimes not even in the body, but that's a matter for another book). I try to hold this image there, this image of an improvement in beauty. I sit with the feeling for a time.

I try to give that feeling a name. "When I hold this idea in my belly, I feel a round tightness." If I have hit upon a useful label, the feeling will deepen, soften, grow warm, or otherwise feel "more right."

Then, I try to give it a name. "Are you plastic surgery?" I ask. I attend to the felt sense I have in my belly—and nothing happens. "Perhaps you're the feeling of redecorating?" This also gets no response, let's say, so I sit a while longer with the feeling. "Is this a new interest in the arts?" While I sit with the feeling, it begins to soften. The more I suspect this, the more it feels right.

Where does this information come from? The body? Perhaps. Or perhaps the body is merely a receiver. Either way, you can get some startling insights this way, even though it's more time consuming than simply memorizing the cards. This is also a useful way to avoid the "reading for oneself" problem, as I've mentioned before: your mind might lie, but the body rarely does.

In a spread, cards in certain positions have salience, as I've mentioned before. It's worthwhile to check for salience elsewhere in the spread, as well. There are two simple techniques for doing so that I use regularly. They both involve a variation of focusing I call "breathing-with."

Breathing-with involves shifting our sensation of breath from our lungs to another body part. For example, we can breathe with our hand. Try this now: begin by focusing on your breath, as you slowly breathe in and out. Now shift your focus on each exhale and inhale to your left hand (left-handed folks may want to swap this, although in my experience it doesn't really matter—you could do this with your foot, I suspect, and get the same results). You should, with some small practice, feel your hand pulse with your breath. When you do, imagine that you are inhaling a light, mist, or "energy" into it with each inhalation. When it begins to feel warm and hypersensitive, you are ready to use it as an intuitive device. Pass it over the spread, and attend to the feeling you're holding in your hand. As it changes, pay attention to the cards it hovers over. This practice can be useful in selecting cards as well; for some spreads, I like to fan the cards out face down and select them this way.

You can also use this with a single tarot card, running your finger over the images until you feel the sensation in your hand change, shift, or increase. The particular part of the image where this occurs takes on increased significance.

Breathing with the eyes involves the same procedure, but in this case you breathe—well, with the eyes. With practice, you may notice objects take on increased "realness" as you look upon them. Those objects are salient.

Finding salient cards can help us parse a string of cards, such as in the Lenormand. We can begin to see which cards can be read as combinations and which cards should be read individually; which cards are topics, and which are comments. Salient cards, which seem "more real" to our breathed-with eyes, or where our hand feels heavier, hotter, or weird, are more likely to be topics.

You can do two other things to improve your intuitive grasp of the situation, and they're both somewhat counterintuitive. Or maybe a better way of putting it (since they're intuitive in the other sense of the word) is that they're not what you might expect. One is to distrust your mind, and the other is to trust your body. If you go by movies, literature, and art, you'll think that divination is a straining activity, wrinkled brow, finger to the forehead. You already know that divination requires intense relaxation, and I've never met what I would regard as a real psychic who put his or her finger to her forehead; most of the people in the occult community I know regard that gesture as ridiculous. The other image we have is the psychic who suddenly gets a flash and runs off to warn the president or find the body. That's usually not the way it works either.

Most psychics worth their salt, in my opinion, carefully consider whether an insight is real or not. It's easy to create false "insights" out of your worries and concerns. If you suddenly have an insight that you'll get in a car accident, rather than stay home and hide from cars, you might consider whether there's another reason you'd have that idea. For example, did you see a TV show with a car accident? Did you read about one, or hear about one on the radio? Are you prone already to be a nervous driver? If you can trace back that insight, even tentatively, to some other inspiration it's probably not really psychic.

This kind of self-awareness requires both a good memory and a mindful attitude. Regular mindfulness meditation in this—as in so many other things—helps. And so does practice. I find it useful practice to trace back, in my mind, the course of a conversation. Another useful practice is to trace your day backwards in your imagination before you go to sleep. This exercise is surprisingly difficult, but trains your mind to find the origin of ideas.

However, with some insights, you try to trace them back and you find that they came out of nowhere. I call it the "brick wall." It's as if an idea appeared through a brick wall, out of nothing. That brick wall is the limits of our analytic mind. Beyond it is the sea of the unconscious. Ideas that come from there aren't all psychic insights, especially if you have a tendency to a bit of neurosis (and really, who doesn't?). But many of them are.

The trick is to trace back an idea to its origin. Is it a rational origin, like you have heard your engine making a funny noise so you feel that your car might break down? Is it an irrational origin, like you heard your neighbor's car broke down and so you're afraid yours will too? Or is it a nonrational origin: you just know, without knowing how, that your car will break down. The nonrational isn't always true, but it's also not to be dismissed as irrational.

Focusing can be aided with a tool that measures your ideomotor response. While that sounds technical, such a tool is actually a simple weight hanging by a thread: a pendulum. I have had my doubts about the pendulum, as I think do many serious occultists. It's surrounded by nonsense and easily falsified claims. As you probably realize, I'm a skeptic and an advocate of bringing critical thinking to magic and divination. I don't think the two approaches are incompatible. So when people make scientific-sounding claims that betray an absolute lack of even basic scientific knowledge, I tend to make myself unpopular by pointing it out. Fortunately, I'm a witty guest and throw a mean dinner party, so I maintain at least some friendships.

I was about eleven, I think, when I first experimented with a pendulum. An article in *Fate* magazine explained how it worked, and I went in search of a piece of string and a nut (the bolt kind, not the food kind) to hang off of it. At first I was pretty impressed with the thing, but then I tried to show it off to my big brother, who filled his office admirably. "You're moving your hand," he pointed out. He was right. I wanted it to work so badly I was making it work. I set aside the pendulum and learned an important lesson about self-deception.

My subsequent experiences with the pendulum proved less than inspiring. I worked in an occult bookstore in my late teens, and we had one customer who used the pendulum the way I had a child: to make it say what he wanted to hear. Since that was normally whether or not he should buy some expensive and foolish thing, we didn't exactly rush to encourage good occult practice.

On the farm, whenever we needed to find some buried thing—a water line, a septic tank (how we lost a septic tank I'll never know), or anything else—we'd pick up a pickax and hold it with the head resting on our palms and the handle sticking straight out, so it could swing right and left. We'd walk forward slowly, and, as we put it, "when it breaks a rib, you found the line." It swung with surprising force.

I thought perhaps the pendulum was bunk, but dowsing wasn't, so I bought a pair of dowsing rods (most of the money I made working at that occult bookstore went back into it pretty quickly, even without a pendulum to encourage my own foolish purchases) and tried them out. They ended up buried in the bottom of a drawer. One would probably need a pickax to find them.

Later, I did what any red-blooded young academic would do. I did some research and found what one often finds in science but what the layman rarely expects: conflicting reports. Several studies showed that some dowsers had a consistent success rate in a contrived experiment. Others showed no such success rate. At this point, we run up against science's problem with the analysis of anomalous data. Anecdotal data fares better: I know many farmers who swear by dowsing. Anecdotal data isn't respected and can be easily explained away, even though it sometimes shouldn't.

James Randi, a famous skeptic, offers a million-dollar prize for anyone displaying scientifically verifiable psychic powers. This prize has never been awarded, and dowsers make the largest category of applicants. Randi explains that dowsing is merely the ideomotor effect, the ability of thoughts to cause small, unconscious movements in the body that influence the swing of a pendulum or a rod. This explanation is demonstrably true. However, it does not explain that people do claim to experience success from it. He admits that most claimants are honest, but nevertheless refuse to face facts. It is clear that self-deception can indeed influence dowsing, and in fact all forms of divination.[23]

Randi's skepticism notwithstanding, other research into anomalous knowledge supports the ability of unconscious bodily motions— the ideomotor effect—to reveal information. For example, Elizabeth Lloyd Mayer describes her own experiences with dowsing in her book *Extraordinary Knowing*. Having lost an expensive musical instrument, she employs the services of a dowser who identifies the street and house of the person who stole it.[24] Yes, "anecdote" is not the singular of "data," but it is not difficult to find people who claim success with dowsing.

What interests me about every study I've seen on the topic is that the researchers take the explanation of the phenomenon from the dowsers as a given. For example, some dowsers claim that they detect the magnetic fields emanating from underground streams. A geologist will tell you that there are very, very few underground streams; most wells take their water from underground aquifers, which are not

---

23. Jeff Wagg, "One Million Dollar Paranormal Challenge," *The James Randi Educational Foundation* (October 2008). http://www.randi.org/site/index .php/1m-challenge.html.

24. Elizabeth Lloyd Mayer, *Extraordinary Knowing: Science, Skepticism, and the Inexplicable Powers of the Human Mind* (NY: Bantam, 2007).

moving water but large rock sponges that ooze water over time. Yet researchers into dowsing set up experiments in which water moves through pipes and dowsers attempt to detect which pipes contain water. If the dowsers are right about the mechanism of their dowsing, then this might work. But what if dowsing works by some other means, such as unconscious detection of geological features that might indicate underground water, or even something more mystical, like unconscious knowledge in the Anima Mundi? And what if one of the features that makes such knowledge available is that it matters, that it means something? A well on a farm is symbolically different from water in a series of pipes. I suspect that any test that does not take into account the symbolic significance of the items sought by dowsing will never accumulate sufficient evidence to convince the skeptic. Actually, I honestly suspect that no study could ever convince the scientific skeptic, because most scientific skeptics are not true skeptics at all, but *a priori* thinkers who have no interest in evidence. But that's another matter.

Using a pendulum in divination, either alone or, better, in synergy with another system, is easy. Details of methods differ from source to source, and some methods are almost computer-like, in which you offer the pendulum programs and complex procedures, but I use a rather simpler method. Franz Bardon offers a no-nonsense approach that he calls "releasing the hand." In this method, you take up the pendulum—you can buy a special one or just tie something heavy to a bit of string—and sit at a table upon which you can rest your elbows. Put the pendulum in one hand and the other hand palm down on the table.[25]

Now, imagine the hand holding the pendulum resting beside the other hand. It may help to stare intently at the pendulum rather than the hand, but imagine your arm sinking down to rest. Try to feel it as vividly as possible. The notion here is that you are symbolically surrendering your hand to the Anima Mundi. Now, ask the pendulum

---

25. Franz Bardon, *Initiation into Hermetics* (Salt Lake City: Merkur Publications, 2005), 150.

to show you the signal it prefers for "ready." For some, this is a short diagonal swing; for others, it is relative stillness. Then ask it to show you "yes." For some, this is a horizontal line; for others, a vertical line or a circle; for me, it is usually a clockwise circle. Ask it to return to "ready," then once it has done so—do not force it—ask it to show you "no." The tricky thing here is to make sure you release the hand and not allow yourself to move your hand consciously. At the same time, you must consciously make no effort to keep your hand still, either. Releasing the hand lets you focus on your "double" hand, and not on the physical one holding the pendulum.

Now you have a simple and easy way of determining yes/no questions. You may also want to set up a signal for "cannot answer" or "that's a silly question." You can also get it to identify numbers and letters, either by having it clink against a glass or by asking it to swing and change its swing in some way when you say the right number or letter.

This last method, by the way, got me four out of five on a pick-five lottery ticket. Or would have, had I bought the ticket. Isn't that convenient? I can win the lottery, but only if I don't play. So much for their slogan. I don't know why it works this way for me, but I suspect it has something to do with my lack of real need, or maybe the tension and anticipation that I feel if I actually intend to play the lottery this way.

The pendulum, however, is notoriously bad at giving you answers for things you don't want to hear. It's like a friend who never wants to give bad news. You could ask it (and by "it" I probably mean the Anima Mundi and your own unconscious) to give you the true answer and not the one you necessarily want. That works, sometimes, but even then I find the pendulum less and less accurate the more I care about the answer. At the same time, if no one cares—if it's something that matters to no one, or means nothing—I rarely get an accurate answer either. It's a strange balancing act. In the web of significance, evidently the hand holding the pendulum cannot sit at the center, but the web must have some center.

How can we use the pendulum with the tarot and the Lenormand? For one thing, if we lay out the Book of Life with the Lenormand, we can move a pendulum over it asking it to indicate what the most significant cards are: what, in other words, are the topics? This can be used to parse a long string of cards, as well, to determine which cards to read in combination and which cards to read individually. The same can be done with the tarot, but with the tarot you can actually use the pendulum to indicate particular symbols on a given card you should pay attention to.

For example, you could hold the pendulum ready in your right hand and run your left forefinger across the card slowly. When the pendulum indicates a "hit"—by changing its swing, for example, or indicating "yes"—look at the symbol your finger is pointing at. With the tarot and the pendulum, you can get a complete and complex reading with just one card, by repeating this with each clarification question. For example, you could run your fingers over the Sun and ask, "What symbol on this card indicates my current situation?" The pendulum might indicate the child, which you could interpret as being a beginner. Again, you might ask with the same card, "And what is that situation changing into?" This time perhaps the pendulum indicates one of the sunflowers, which always turn their heads to face the sun: you are becoming a follower, perhaps. "What would be my most effective course of action?" you might ask. Now, the pendulum indicates a hit when your finger points to the eyes of the sun-figure. You need to open your eyes to see that you're being dazzled.

We can also use the pendulum to double-check our interpretations. "Does 36–Cross here indicate worry? Suffering? Religion?" That has its place, especially when reading for yourself. The pendulum checks and balances the cards, which balance the pendulum's tendency to tell us what we want to hear. Both act as aids to our intuition, like focusing and other meditative techniques. At the root of it, the pendulum and the cards are tools. But we scorn the use of tools at our own expense; if you doubt that, try pounding in a nail without a hammer or screwing in a screw with your fingers.

Intuitive reading is a matter of practice more than a matter of discussion, which means you need to practice it to get good at it, not just read about it. Therefore, other than the suggestions for exercises that I've listed above, there isn't much else to say about developing your intuition of the cards. The best way to do so is to practice the intuitive exercises above, and create some of your own. An attitude of playfulness is worth a lot more than the serious glowering over dusty tomes that fills our media depictions of occultism. One of the most talented psychics I have ever known was a playful, witty, profane and hilarious woman who relied on the cheesiest oracle deck she could find and forced it into uses more refined and intuitive than any tarot reader I've ever met. She read intuitively, ignoring the instruction booklet and, sometimes, the cards themselves. The playful psychic isn't exactly a common archetype, but it might be a useful one to explore for those who wish to read intuitively rather than by-the-book.

CHAPTER XII

Collaborative Reading

As I explained in the introduction, there are two models of divination: the transmission model and the construction model. In the transmission model, the diviner gets the message from the Anima Mundi and passes it on, as if it is a package or box of information. Errors, if they occur, are attributed to a failure to properly protect the contents in transmission.

In this model, the diviner is a channel and the querent is the receiver.

As models go, this fits our instinct about how we deal with information, how we communicate it and manipulate it. We conceive of information as a substance that can be poured into containers—our heads, a book, a computer, a set of cards—and extracted from those containers if you just know how to squeeze them the right way. We fill up our heads on information, pour it out of mouths and into our ears, as if we are complex vases.

The problem with this model is that it doesn't fit reality. No model does, really, but this one leaves some big gaps. For example, if information is a substance we pour into containers, where does it come from? Is there just a sea of information somewhere out there that we dip into? If so, where does that sea come from? And if we can simply transfer information from one head to another, why—even in mundane situations of communication—does that transmission end up garbled, not some of the time, but all of the time? Why is something always "missing in translation?" If, every time we sent a package of cookies to a friend, three of the cookies were missing and one had been replaced with a piece of fried calamari, we'd be darned suspicious of the company we hired to deliver the package. We might even suspect that they didn't deliver the package we sent at all, but replaced it with something else. Yet this equivalent thing happens nearly every time we communicate: something always goes missing, something always goes wrong. This happens so often we have built communicative strategies to correct for such errors—"I'm sorry." "Pardon me?" "Come again?" "I missed that." "Did you mean … ?"

The second model of communication, one more useful in some cases than the transmission model, is the constructivist model. In this model, instead of sending a box of cookies to my friend, I send a recipe for cookies. The exact shape and even flavor of the cookies my friend gets are up to him. Maybe I call for raw cocoa, but the brand I use and the brand my friend has in his pantry are different. Maybe I suggest a cup of whole milk, but all he's got is skim. I can't know what's in his fridge before I send the recipe: I can just hope that he'll figure it out and come up with something like my cookies.

And, usually, he does. The differences are not errors in transmission, but a function of having differently stocked fridges. Our heads are kitchens, stocked with different goods. I can never know what ingredients are in your mental fridge, nor can I know how hot your mental oven runs. But I can give you a recipe that constructs a particular idea in my head, and hope that you can bake a similar, although never the same, idea in your head. I am not communicating a *thing* to my friend at all: not sending a box of cookies, but the directions for making such a box of cookies. Perhaps my friend's cookies will not turn out like mine, but if so, that's not a failure on either of our parts: it might just be because his kitchen is different.

I desperately want to make cookies right now, but let's continue with our theorizing and we can eat dessert later.

When we use a transmission model of divination, we create a hierarchy in which the diviner reads and the querent listens. Sure, the querent may ask questions, but those questions provoke not discussion, but lecture. This is a top-down model of divination; the message comes from on high, and trickles through the diviner to the querent. It is, to continue our metaphor, as if the Anima Mundi hands a package of information off to the diviner, who hands it over to the querent.

I don't mean to condemn such a model. It has, after all, served most diviners well, including the famous Mlle. Lenormand. And it can be helpful for the querent to hear the past, present, and future analyzed and given a voice. There's also some emotional benefit, I believe, to the experience of having an authority to go to for advice, one who speaks *ex cathedra*. However, this model of top-down lecturing isn't always the most appropriate, and it also is open to abuse. It's easy for an unscrupulous diviner, for example, to pull a hoax or fraud on a receptive querent. If I tell you there's a "dark cloud" (a favorite phrase of frauds) around you, and I must burn a specially blessed candle worth several hundred dollars to get rid of it, perhaps you will believe me if you're disposed to accept me as an authority who speaks for the Anima Mundi. That would be a pity.

A constructivist view of divination looks a bit different. Here, instead of a top-down line of transmission from the Anima Mundi, as if the Anima Mundi is passing cookies down the line, the querent and diviner come together around the cards. And suddenly, the terms "querent" and "diviner" cease to mean much, because both are asking the questions, both are giving the answers. Here we have a center-out model: the recipe lies on the table, and both people collaborate on constructing meanings from it.

Notice the plural, too: meanings. Because now we have twice the fridge space, twice the counter space, and two ovens. We can make many different batches of cookies where once there was one. Where once a single authority spoke the meaning of the cards, now two voices come together in dialogue to construct meanings, some of which might fit, some of which might not.

The master of this constructivist method of reading is Mary K. Greer, and her book *21 Ways of Reading Tarot Cards* is a *sine qua non* for cartomancers of all stripes, not just tarot card readers.[26] I can't duplicate her work here, or even do full justice to it. But to attempt a summary, her general tendency is to look at the cards as building blocks of meaning, rather than set signs with definite meanings. We can do something similar with other divination systems, such as the Lenormand.

Once you lay out the cards for a querent, instead of saying what the cards mean, simply name and describe them. For example, a traditional simple reading for a querent might go like this:

Q: I want to know if this investment will work out.
Cards: 23–Mouse, 33–Key, 5–Tree
R: I think probably so. I see a little worry and concern, but it's sort of fated: that's what Key followed by Tree usually means.

A constructivist reading would look different, in that the reader would ask as many questions as the querent.

Q: I want to know if this investment will work out.
Cards: 23–Mouse, 33–Key, 5–Tree
R: These are Mouse, Key, and Tree. What do you think of when you see Mouse?
Q: I guess I have to laugh. We call our accountant "Mouse." He's little and squirrelly.
R: And Key?
Q: Well, he's kind of key to the whole thing, I suppose. It was his suggestion we do this thing.
R: What about Tree?

---

26. Mary K. Greer, *21 Ways to Read a Tarot Card* (Woodbury, MN: Llewellyn, 2007).

Q: That's actually funny. I was concerned about the environmental impact. Do you think this is saying it's going to be okay, or not?

R: Sometimes, Key is like an exclamation point.

Q: So it's saying that the environmental impact will be really important?

R: Maybe.

As you can see, there are fewer certainties, but it's a lot more interesting of a reading. The most interesting thing is when a querent says "I have no idea what that might mean." At that point, a reader might prod gently by offering one or two possible meaning of the cards. But notice the reader isn't so much reading the cards as he or she is taking the querent's hand and teaching him or her to read.

One of the things I like a lot about this constructivist approach is that it empowers the querent and can be life-changing. Yet not every reading is appropriate for such a thing. I sometimes read at parties, and I wouldn't want to do it there: after all, who wants to have a life-changing insight at a dinner party? But at other times, when people come to me specifically for readings about events that concern them, it can be a great way to empower people to understand and maybe change their own lives.

Be prepared to deal with real issues when you read cards this way for other people. At this point, you've left behind the "psychic" label and become a sort of ancillary lay therapist. However, keep in mind that you're probably not qualified (unless, of course, you are) to be a therapist. You probably lack the training, and should therefore resist the temptation to step in and "help" someone work through their ideas and issues. It's their job to do so, not yours, and you mustn't rob them of the opportunity once you give it to them.

Also, be ready to offer sympathy and support; after all, most people don't come to a reader because everything is fine. They often come because things are not fine, and they need to work through those problems. They may even beg you for advice; the best and kindest thing you can do is just lead them through the cards, as a way for them to work through their own problems. At this point, you're engaging more in a kind of counseling than psychic prediction, and that's fine. Most people need quite a bit less prediction than introspection. Just make sure you don't call yourself a counselor unless you're legally qualified to do so in your jurisdiction.

And if you aren't prepared to help querents in difficult situations like this, you should probably give up the idea of reading for others, at least professionally. There's no shame in that, and reading for oneself and one's circle of friends is also rewarding.

So the constructivist approach is useful when reading for others. What about when reading for oneself? How can you guide yourself through the cards in a similar way? After all, you obviously see only what you see. But there are several techniques you can use that will help you approach the cards more constructively.

For example, a common practice among cartomancers is to draw "a card for the day." I recommend this practice, both as a way to learn the deck as well as a way to prepare for the day. It also helps get over the fear of some cards that some readers have (I loathe drawing 36–Cross, to this day—but really, the misery it predicts is really never all *that* bad). But its real use comes when you regard the cards in a constructivist way rather than as transmissions of packaged information.

It helps to do this with a written journal of some kind, even if it's informal. Begin by drawing a single card and writing the name at the top of a page of your journal. You'll want to make two columns. On the left, list the meaning as you understand it, and then free-associate a bit. Fill this side with ideas of how the card might fit your life: the names of people whom it might indicate or describe, the kinds of situations that it might be relevant to. Then, on the right-hand side of the page, write the date you drew it. At the end of the day, write any events that fit the card on the right.

If you do this regularly, you'll eventually have pages for most if not all of the cards in the deck. You'll also have a lot of material from which you can construct meanings. Much more importantly, you'll have practiced the process again and again, and can use it even on yourself when you need it.

The real trick to doing a constructivist reading with yourself is to talk to yourself and write to yourself. You need both. Writing down your interpretations, even in outline form, keeps you honest. It's harder to self-deceive if you have the reading laid out before you in black and white. Similarly, if you can bring yourself to talk to yourself out loud, even when alone (especially when alone), you'll be less likely to gloss over details that would otherwise catch your eye.

When reading for yourself, you're likely to run into the issue of self-deception. When reading for someone else, it's easier to say "this card means a difficult time is coming," or even "this card means good news" but when reading for yourself, it's easy to try to gloss over the bad cards, or worse, catastrophize them.

The simplest way I've found to overcome these self-deceptive tendencies is to pretend that you're not reading for yourself. You're reading for a querent much like you; would you tell that querent that this card is unmitigated disaster? Probably not. And would you tell the querent to ignore that unpleasant-looking card? Probably not. Why treat yourself differently from a querent? If you read the cards aloud, and speak your meanings so that you can hear them, it's easier to do this: to separate yourself from your reading long enough to be objective.

The process of constructivist reading for oneself looks like this:

1. Lay out the cards after your usual ritual.

2. Then focus on the first card, name it, and ask aloud, "What could this card mean? How might it be relevant?"

3. Speak a few possibilities, even if they aren't altogether motivated by the card alone: "It's the Hierophant. It seems he's trying to teach, but the acolytes before him aren't really listening. They're paying more attention to who is he than what he's saying. I wonder if that describes the situation at work . . ."

4. Brainstorm possibilities, jotting them down as you go.

5. You can check them by focusing on them, finding which of them offers a "felt sense" of rightness and which do not.

6. Alternately, or in addition, you can use the pendulum as a way to check your body's reaction to possible interpretations.

The goal of constructivist reading, whether for yourself or others, is not to predict the future or arrive at accurate facts, but to gain insight and meaning from the current situation. Described that way, perhaps it sounds less flashy or impressive than prediction, but one of the insights we are inclined to glean is insight into the future. Moreover, what's more impressive? Predicting the future or understanding oneself? One can maybe help you plan for future advantages; the other can help you grow into a better person in every sense.

CHAPTER XIII

Symbolic Interaction Between
the Lenormand and Tarot

As explained earlier, the tarot is a mystical communication with
the Anima Mundi, encoding the symbols used by occultists to
communicate with her since ancient times. Or, more likely, those
symbols were deliberately introduced when the tarot was repurposed
from a card game to a magical tool of divination.

But when we look at the images on the Petit Lenormand, we find
very little reflection of Fludd's Mirror of Nature. At least at first. We
can impose some obvious associations with astrological symbols on
the cards. For example, 34–Fish can be associated with Pisces. And
the astrological associations of 31–Sun and 32–Moon are self-explan-
atory. But the two symbol systems do not fit together as nicely as the
tarot fits with astrology; there is a lot more blending of symbols and
clearly little in the way of conscious, deliberate alignment with the
Mirror of Nature.

There are obvious and not-so-obvious reasons for this. The most
obvious reason is that the thirty-six cards of the Lenormand were
not invented by an occultist. Neither were the twenty-two cards of

the major arcana, but occultists took it upon themselves to stick their fingers in that particular pot and stir. And those occultists were well-educated men and women, some of them with rather a lot of money. Those who repurposed the Petit Lenormand for its current divinatory uses (the original use of the card game for divination is much less elaborate than current practices) were not well educated in the same sense. They probably hadn't read Homer in the original Greek or spent a year traveling the continent with their father's money. I'm not saying they were illiterate, or even impoverished, but they were educated by a different standard: a practical, daily standard. On the other hand, even though the founders of the occult tarot weren't all wealthy, they were educated. Antoine Court de Gébelin, for example, went to seminary and was trained as a pastor.

The symbols of the Lenormand, unlike those of the tarot, refer not to archetypal themes like "Justice" but to everyday occurrences in the life of the eighteenth- and nineteenth-century gentry of Europe. Consider card 27–Letter for a moment. Letters were the lifeblood of the eighteenth-century gentry. It was not uncommon for a woman to send several letters throughout the day and receive quite a few in response. So important and central was this system of messaging that until recently England delivered the post several times a day. One of the reasons for this central importance of letters was the cloistered life of women. I'm not suggesting that all women were locked up (some were, actually, but not all). But women did set certain times at which they were "at home" and available to receive visitors. Such visitors might come from afar for the specific purpose of seeing a woman—such as 1–Rider. A woman had to be home at those times, but at the same time, she needed to arrange other visits with other women. The social network had to be maintained, so communication had to be continually maintained as well. Eighteenth- and nineteenth-century women wrote letters the way that many young men and women now send text messages, and in nearly the same volume (if with better spelling and never while driving).

Notice, too, that card 25–Ring is different from card 24–Heart. Love and marriage were not always the same thing. In some senses

25–Ring is a card of finance, which survives in its contemporary meaning of "contract." Marriage *is* a contract, and for many women of this era, the only contract with which they could hope to make a living. Let the men worry about airy philosophical concepts like "Justice" and "Temperance." Women needed to concern themselves with their financial as well as domestic future. It's telling that 25–Ring traditionally could mean "a proposal," but VII–The Lovers traditionally meant "a choice." It is the man with his tarot deck who chooses, the woman with the Lenormand who receives the proposal.

So it stands to reason that the Lenormand would not concern itself with the ceremonial magic and complex astrology to which some men and women bent their time. Obviously, a lot of astrological symbolism and a lot of Fludd's Mirror of Nature show up here; it's because it's actually reflected unconsciously rather than deliberately designed by occultists. There were female occultists, many of them quite educated and some of them contributed to the development of the tarot. But the Lenormand was used for ordinary questions and ordinary concerns.

In practice, however, so is the tarot. Pick up any book on the tarot and you'll see a list of everyday meanings even for the major arcana. After all, how many archetypal life-changing events occur on a daily basis? Not many. Even the wealthy, Latin-reading, brandy-sipping, velvet-coat-wearing men of the Golden Dawn were probably excited to get some mail.

Yet there are patterns of symbols in the Lenormand. I haven't seen much discussion of them in the few texts available on the Lenormand in English or Spanish. (I am, sadly, unable to read German—which is a pity, because the Lenormand is popular in Germany.) For example, each of the cards, as explained above, is associated traditionally with a particular playing card. It seems these traditional associations might have some significance, and in fact we can trace back some systems of meaning to early systems of reading the cards.

For example, consider the court cards of the spades. We have 13–Child, 9–Flowers, and 30–Lily. Each of these cards can represent a person: a child, a young woman, and an old man. The spades' court cards share the meaning of "time." This meaning doesn't carry into the other cards in the suit, however, although spades do often deal with issues of intellect and communication and travel. Similarly, almost all the "negative" cards are clubs. Many of the hearts deal with friendship and love. And diamonds often deal with money and fortune. Finally, we see that two of the aces are signifiers. At some point in the development of the Lenormand, these images were the meaning attributed to a thirty-six-card deck of playing cards.[27] Yet this association is loose; we would expect 8–Coffin to be a club, but it's a diamond. And we would probably expect 25–Ring to be a diamond, but it's the Ace of Clubs.

But why are these cards not in order? We would expect them to be numbered, perhaps, according to their playing card sequence, but instead they're numbered seemingly randomly, as if they've been previously shuffled. There are, however, some patterns in this seemingly random numbering as well. The cards 28–Gentleman and 29–Lady follow each other, and 35–Ring follows 34–Heart: marriage follows love, ideally. And 31–Sun precedes 32–Moon. Of course, in the original game, this order was simply the order in which the cards were laid down, so that one could travel over them by throwing dice. There has been no effort to put esoteric significance into this order, as there has with the tarot.

What we also don't find, overall, is a clear astrological association. The keys of two, three, four, seven, and twelve appear to be nearly absent. We do have thirty-six cards, which is three times the key of twelve. But laying the cards out in that pattern, three rows of twelve, does not reveal much insight, really. Similarly, we could try to arrange them according to the decans of the zodiac, ten-degree divisions of each of the signs. But doing so also seems to make little sense.

So where are the reflections of this Mirror of Nature in our humble little deck? Unlike the tarot, no one seems to have sat down and made the thing conform to the model of the universe depicted in

---

27. http://lenormanddictionary.blogspot.com/p/lenormand-suits.html, accessed April 2, 2013.

Fludd. But if the Anima Mundi is using these cards to communicate with us, surely some of these symbols should appear.

It might help to analyze the cards by the surface feature of the symbols employed. Then we might see, at least, how the maker of the Petit Lenormand divided up her world.

External World	Animals	Objects / Tools
6. Clouds	7. Snake	8. Coffin
16. Stars	12. Birds	10. Scythe
20. Garden	14. Fox	11. Whip
21. Mountain	15. Bear	24. Heart
22. Crossroads	17. Stork	25. Ring
31. The Sun	18. Dog	26. Book
32. The Moon	23. Mice	27. Letter
	34. Fish	33. Key
		35. Anchor
		36. Cross

People	Plants	Edifices / Machines
1. Rider	2. Clover	3. Ship
13. Child	5. Tree	4. House
28. Gentleman	9. Flowers	19. Tower
29. Lady	30. Lily	

Some of these attributions are, admittedly, a bit sketchy. A heart as an object is crowbarred in there, I'll admit. But in general this chart reveals that the creator of the Lenormand relied on a limited number of symbolic domains. These domains are particularly heavy in familiar, daily objects. A woman in a drawing room probably had little experience with anchors, but she surely knew very well the nature of keys, books, letters, crosses, and rings. Notice the heavy weight of symbols from nature: clouds, mountains, plants, and animals. Yet even so, there's a sense of randomness, of disorder, behind these symbols.

Romanticism

How do we account for this disarray of symbols? We have the tarot, which began as a catch-as-catch-can collection of cards for card games, and settled finally into a carefully constructed set of symbols based, as we have seen, on the ideas of late-Renaissance Neoplatonism. But what principle governs the seeming melange of the cards of the Lenormand?

It's important to understand that the eighteenth and nineteenth centuries in Europe marked a paradigm shift in modes of thought. Old ways of understanding the world gave way, rather suddenly, to a new way of thinking. Often referred to as "the Enlightenment," this new mode of thought privileged "rationality" and "reason" over emotion and authority. Obviously, in the history of human ideas, this new notion is just a dusted-off version of old ideas, but now scholars had the ability to distribute and share rational observations of the world with each other, and a foundation of philosophical skepticism that allowed them to test ideas empirically. The roots of this revolution in thinking fed institutions and movements as diverse as science, politics, and even—a bit later—literature and art in the form of realism and naturalism.

But as always happens in a revolution of ideas, there was a counter-revolution. Actually, there were two: the first is the return to the Neoplatonism of the Renaissance, as we've already seen, which fueled a small occult revival in the nineteenth century and influenced the symbols of the tarot. This looking backward to older philosophies is sometimes called Neoclassicism, although the original Neoplatonism occurred a bit later than the classical era. Nevertheless, one way of responding to the new "rationality" was to look to the past, for other ways of knowing. The other, larger and more influential counter to Enlightenment thinking is called Romanticism.

Romanticism began as a movement in Germany and England before spreading to the rest of Europe. It met head-on Napoleon's efforts to rule France and conquer Europe, and in that crucible took on an interesting new form in France, feeding the streams of classical liberalism as well as a kind of conservative populism. I called it a movement, but Romanticism was never deliberately organized so much as organically sprouted from the fertile soil of an industrializing Europe. Therefore, Romantics often seem to espouse contradictory ideas.

For example, the highest form of humanity for the Romantic is the creative genius, transforming the torments of his or her tortured existence into art. At the same time, however, the simplicity of rural life, its orderly regularity (as perceived from the vantage of a city garrett, of course), was held up as an example of spiritual richness. What can you do, then, as a Romantic, if you idealize the wild Lord Byron flitting about the world being tortured, drunk, and—well—laid? You also idealize the farmer with his poor dirty hands at the plough. So, to reconcile these two heroes, you declare the farmer a kind of genius. Genius, then, can spring up anywhere, like a weed: this is the foundation of Romanticism's liberalism.

What mattered to the Romantic, what was of value, was not reason per se. It was the passionate realization of awe in the face of nature and the power of imagination. The poet held a mirror up to nature; that was his or her job. This creation of art reflecting nature was an act of supreme courage, because nature was both nourishing and awful (in the original sense of the word—it caused awe) to the soul. It was also a lonely act: a single genius must do this, not a committee or council.

The Romantic attitude toward knowledge reflected this individuality. It was not through community testing and peer review that one knows something: one knows something by going and seeing. Emotional experience, intuition, and personal revelation were the sources of knowledge, not mathematical reasoning or logic. Imagination, above all, was the power that drove the Romantic genius.

Nature, for the Romantic, is the source of all knowledge and wisdom. If you see a painting with wild craggy mountains jutting over a stormy ocean, perhaps with a single indistinct figure atop it holding on to his hat, you likely are looking at a Romantic painting. Other technical characteristics also mark art as Romantic: the brush strokes are heavy and textured, there's less effort to depict reality and more emotion and passion, and so forth. But ultimately all of these characteristics come back to the idea that nature is the source of the good: humans are by nature good, and if a human follows his or her natural passions, good will come of it. Those who follow their passions and end up doing evil are really following artificial passions, imposed on them by society, wittingly or not.

We see this idea as well in literature of the time. In England, William Blake writes, "If it were not for the Poetic or Prophetic Character the Philosophic & Experimental would soon be at the ratio of all things, and stand still, unable to do other than repeat the same dull round over again."[28] This is both a criticism of the rationalism (the "ratio") of the enlightenment and the mechanism of the Neoplatonic spheres; if we rely on philosophy and experimentation, our actions are mechanical, going "the same dull round over again" with no meaning. It is the individual's prophetic or poetic genius that gives meaning to the discoveries of science and the speculations of philosophy.

Where a transcendent deity in Neoplatonism sends down a chain of increasingly more immanent manifestations to Earth, finally culminating in the Anima Mundi, in Romanticism the divine is seen in nature herself, and in the individual. The Anima Mundi is, herself, nature, and God is often seen as the universe itself. The Romantics begin to imagine God as immanent, as present in the world as we see it, not separate from it, and so needing no intermediaries. What we talk to when we divine from the Romantic perspective is the divine in ourselves, and we do so out of "enthusiasm," in its original etymological sense: the God within.

The Lenormand oracle was defined, not in response to Neoclassical ideas or Neoplatonic ideas, but in response to Romantic ideas.

The Romantic imagination resists systematization. By this I mean the Romantic is likely to walk by church on Sunday whistling, just to show that he can worship God wherever he likes, without formula or ritual. The Romantic does not want tables or charts; who

---

28. William Blake, *The Portable Blake*, ed. Alfred Kazin (NY: Viking, 1971), 77.

needs such things when nature herself gives abundantly of her knowledge? The ordering, structure, and symbols of the Lenormand reflect, at every turn, the Romantic spirit of the deck.

If we look at the distribution of the symbols in the deck, we can see this Romantic influence clearly. We see, for example, that the vast majority of the cards represent plants, the external world or nature, or animals. Only three cards represent human structures, and only four cards represent people. The category of tools or objects is dominated by objects of an agrarian nature, or symbolic of Romantic import, such as the key and anchor. We have a deck that represents not the astrological cycles of the Anima Mundi, but the genius of daily life and imagination idealized by the Romantic movement.

The Tarot and the Lenormand in Synergy

But how does this set of symbols interact with the tarot and how can the symbols of the tarot help us learn to read the Lenormand and vice versa? In two ways: through those astrological associations listed above, as well as by means of deliberate invocation of these daily objects in the cards themselves. In other words, from the perspective of the Neoplatonic top-down structure of the universe, or the Romantic immanent spiritual view. Can we reconcile the two, or must we choose?

If you look at the major arcana of a tarot deck based on Waite's design, you'll see a number of ordinary objects. These objects appear as emblems, decorations, but rarely as the central figures of the cards themselves. But it is clear that the makers of the tarot lived with these daily objects and regarded them as symbolically significant. Not all of the symbols of the Lenormand appear in the major arcana of the tarot (the anchor is hard to find), but most of them do. And those that don't often have clear astrological associations connected to the astrological significance of the tarot cards. For example, the Hanged Man is sometimes associated with water, because it is assigned to the Hebrew letter *mem*, which means "water." Similarly, one of its meanings—standstill, waiting—fits well with 35–Anchor.

Every card of the major arcana echoes the everyday concerns of
the Lenormand, which means most cards in the Lenormand have a
major arcana card (sometimes several) that rules them. One can think
of the major arcana of the tarot as representing archetypal ideas and
the Lenormand cards as representing their manifestation in ordinary,
day-to-day life. The correspondence isn't (and cannot be) a one-for-
one correspondence, but even the concentration of symbols on certain
cards can reveal some interesting things about the way these archetypes manifest. After all, some archetypes are more fertile than others.

Major arcana card 0–the Fool, for example, contains 18–Dog, 31–
Sun, and 18–Mountain. We also see a flower, perhaps indicative of
9–Flowers, although that's perhaps a stretch. The dog here seems to
goad the fool on, and also acts as his enthusiastic companion. The sun
is a promise of success to come, and the mountains in the distance
represent the obstacles he will face as he continues on his journey.
We'll see those mountains in the backgrounds of a lot of cards.

In the Magician, we see 30–Lily and 7–Snake. The magician is
girded with the slyness of the serpent—this recalls some early forms
of the cards, in which the magician was a juggler or mountebank. But
below him grow the lilies of contemplation. The magician is also, in
some systems, the male querent, and therefore card 28–Gentleman.

The High Priestess, like the Magician, is the female querent in
some old methods of reading, and thus contains 29–Lady. But she
also holds 26–Book, although perhaps it is 27–Letter. In some decks,
she holds a bound book. But in the Waite, she holds a scroll, which
could be either. There is some ambiguity and secrecy in the priestess.
Does she hold universal wisdom or a personal message? We also see
with her 36–Cross and 32–Moon. She represents the burden of faith,
as well as the imaginative powers of the moon. Here's a place where
astrological significance meets the iconography of the card: II–The
High Priestess is associated with the moon, as is the Lenormand 32–
Moon card.

The most obvious Lenormand symbol in the Empress is 24–
Heart, which makes sense as she represents the emotional faculty. But
she's also sitting before a 5–Tree. As mother of all, she guards the

health of the world. We also see a multitude of flowers, which recall 9–Flowers, although that symbol will reappear throughout the major arcana.

The Emperor gives us little to work with other than the 21–Mountain in his background. But the Hierophant who follows him offers us 33–Key and 36–Cross. We see here the burden of dogma, but also the keys to the kingdom.

The Lovers is an interesting card from the perspective of the Lenormand because of its cluster of negative symbols. We have some good symbols: 31–Sun, for example. But we also have 21–Mountain between the two lovers, 7–Snake behind the woman (an obvious reference to Eden, but so is the Lenormand card), and 6–Clouds. These symbols are practically a catalogue of what can go wrong. There are obstacles and confusion and deception in love, but over all shines the sun, and the blessing of the angel. Here's a case where the Lenormand symbols enrich the reading of the card: we can see the nature of the choice offered by the angel: overcome the obstacle between you, through clouds of confusion and temptation, and perhaps you'll achieve success. But perhaps not: you cannot know. You must choose blindly.

The Chariot is a bit more straightforward. We see 19–Tower and 16–Star. You might also think of him as 1–Rider. He moves forward with his internal authority of mind.

Justice is the first card in which the Lenormand really seems to have taken a vacation. We could argue, perhaps, that 10–Scythe partakes of the quality of the sword: it represents decisions. It's interesting, by the way, that "decision" comes from a root meaning "to cut." But ultimately, there's not much in this card that appears in the Lenormand.

The Hermit, also, is sparsely colonized by the Lenormand: he has a single 16–Star in his lantern. The Wheel of Fortune, however, is a bit more productive. We have again 7–Snake, as well as 6–Clouds. Fortune is deceptive and uncertain. We also have 26–Book, four of them to be precise, to represent the secret nature of our fate.

Strength also has the ubiquitous 21–Mountain in the background. Here, it reveals the nature of the enterprise: to overcome obstacles by strength. What kind of strength is revealed by the presence of 9–Flowers? The power of beauty and grace.

I've already addressed the possible association of 36–Anchor with the Hanged Man, but I'll also point out that he rests on a 5–Tree, a symbol of spiritual and physical growth.

The next card, Death, is symbolically chockablock with Lenormand symbols. First, we have 1–Rider, the visitor who cannot be denied. In older decks, he wields a 10–Scythe. This the grim cutting off of life. But behind the 19–Towers in the distance rises, or sets, the 31–Sun. And before the grim rider stands a 13–Child. Even in this ending there is hope for tomorrow, and this cutting off itself may be a blessing.

Temperance offers us 22–Crossroad (or, at least, a road) as well as 31–Sun again—although that sun might be more accurately described as a 25–Ring. The multiple choices of the crossroads become unified into a single whole in the form of the ring; this sense of completion occurs also in the water 30–Lily that grow behind the angel.

The Devil does not contain any Lenormand images, but the Tower practically *is* a Lenormand symbol: 19–Tower. But we also see 6–Clouds in the back: here is authority toppled, and confusion. This combination of Lenormand symbols spells anarchy.

The next three cards are also Lenormand images, but they contain some other Lenormand symbols as well. For example, the Star also contains 5–Tree, as well as perhaps 17–Stork, if you're willing to squint. Here is the hope of spiritual change. The Moon, aside from 32–Moon, also has 18–Dog, 14–Fox, and if you're willing to stretch definitions, 34–Fish: these animals symbolize companions, deception, and adventure, all available interpretations of the tarot Moon. Moreover, we also get 19–Tower and 22–Crossroad. These two towers appear again and again in the tarot: they represent a distant gate into a destination, but in the Lenormand they're symbols of authority and institutional power. Finally, in the Sun, we get not just 31–Sun, but also 1–Rider, 13–Child, and our common 9–Flowers. This is the coming of innocence and beauty, under the blessings of the Sun.

Judgement is another card filled with Lenormand symbols. Some 8–Coffins float on a sea before a 21–Mountain range, while an angel blows a trumpet decorated with a 36–Cross through some 6–Clouds. Here we have repeated Lenormand symbols of ending and beginning again: the future is uncertain, and we must face it with faith, but we can be sure there are obstacles. However, we arise, transformed, to meet it.

The final card, the World, again seems sparsely populated with the Lenormand. We have 6–Clouds, but they are light, not dark. And the four cherubic figures which we have seen again and again, I am loath to attribute to Lenormand symbols (an eagle is a bird, but it doesn't seem to me to be a 12–Bird). One symbol that does occur, however, is 25–Ring, a sign of completion in which the hermaphrodite dances.

We get to the end of the major arcana and see that some are heavy with Lenormand symbols, others less so. The most interesting thing for me is that these symbols in the tarot often mean the same thing as they do in the Lenormand. In other words, it's as if Pamela Colman Smith spoke the language of its symbols well enough to incorporate them into her tarot. Or perhaps the tarot, like the planets in Fludd's diagram, sent rays into the physical world that manifested as these ordinary objects, reflected more directly in the Lenormand. Or, as another possibility, the Romantic associations of these symbols so permeated the culture that Pamela Colman Smith used them instinctively, thus joining the Neoclassical and Neoplatonic tarot to the Romantic Lenormand.

For all practical purposes, the question of whether the Anima Mundi is an emanation of a higher, transcendent deity or an immanent deity in her own regard is a moot one. These philosophical roots help us understand these two different plants, but we don't need to cleave to one or the other to use either deck. I am inclined to think that both are true, from different perspectives, and neither contains the whole truth of reality.

Fortune-Telling and Divination

Another supposed difference between the tarot and the Lenormand is the purpose of the decks. The tarot is seen by some as a source for contemplation and meditation, the Lenormand for divination and fortune-telling. However, this distinction, too, deconstructs itself when closely examined. Some magicians make a distinction between divination and fortune-telling. Divination, for them, is a divine act of gaining knowledge. Fortune-telling is, at its best, a means of gaining information about everyday events. At its worst, fortune-telling is mere entertainment or fraud. The prototypical example is astrology. Divination by astrology is a complex process involving the calculation of the positions of numerous planetary bodies. To do it properly requires knowing both the exact place and time of birth. Fortune telling by astrology looks more like newspaper horoscopes, which simply assume—ridiculously—that everyone with the same sun sign will experience the same events. Most newspaper horoscopes are written by people with no actual interest in or knowledge of astrology at all, but even those who are meticulous enough to calculate transits must realize the broad brush with which they are painting. In some sense, then, this distinction is justified because it permits us to point to things that are useful and things that are not.

Yet the questions asked of diviners and fortune-tellers throughout history have often been exactly the same. It appears that people want to know relatively few things: about love, about money, and about their children. The only difference in questions between those offered at the Oracle of Delphi and those asked a modern fortune-teller is the scope. Someone may want to know whether to expand his business; someone may ask the Oracle at Delphi how to conquer a neighboring city. In both cases, the questions are similar: how can I increase my domain?

The distinction between divination and fortune-telling cannot rest squarely on method, either. After all, the Order of the Golden Dawn holds the tarot in high esteem, but for most of the cards' history the cards were entertainment: first a game, and then a parlor trick. Perhaps we can rest the distinction between the two on the intent of the querent. If the querent intends only to be entertained, then he or she gets fortune-telling. If he or she intends to be informed, then we call the act divination. However, many people perform fortune-telling at home for entertainment and nevertheless take the advice of the cards or the tea leaves seriously.

We could also rest the distinction on the explanation for the act. The word "divination" implies some interaction with divine beings: gods or spirits at the very least. Fortune-telling does not, necessarily. But this distinction isn't fully satisfactory because many fortune-tellers make at least some gesture toward piety. And some diviners do not.

What we end up with, ultimately, is a bag of unsatisfactory explanations clinking around. What we really need to is to cut through the issue and ask if the distinction is really useful, and if so, for what?

Unfortunately, the distinction may have much more to do with social class than any inherent nature of the act. Essentially, a divination costs more. Perhaps the distinction is only useful if we want to distinguish between what the upper classes do, and what the lower classes do. The issue is complicated by the fact that magic, too, has its social classes. The distinctions between high and low magic, for example, parallel a historical distinction between ceremonial magic and folk magic. Folk magic includes such practices as drawing hex signs on barns, or "laying tricks" in the Hoodoo tradition. The misconception is that high magic focuses, like divination, on loftier goals: union with God, for example, and low magic, like fortune-telling, focuses on matters of daily practical import: getting a good crop, making sure your man isn't stepping out, and getting the hen to lay. If you read the account of any of the magical Lodge Wars, long and tedious affairs involving various supposedly lofty magicians throwing curses at each other, you can see that they wouldn't be allowed in the kitchen of any respectable farm wife. Similarly, it is possible with a little looking to find loftier spiritual goals among the daily work of folk magic.

Therefore, I'm suspicious of the distinction. When I mention "fortune-telling," therefore, I am not pointing out a distinction I believe in, but one that others use. And when I use the word, I mean to use it from their perspective. If this were a more scholarly work, I might carefully put quotation marks around every occurrence of the word, to make that sense of it plain, but I find that practice annoying and precious even in scholarly works. So I won't do it here. If it would help you to keep in mind that the distinction is a troubled one, feel free to pencil in quotation marks around the word.

There is a difference between foretelling and commenting, however, that we could map onto fortune-telling and divination. Foretelling is attempting to predict the future, while commenting is simply offering insight on the present or past. It's easier, philosophically, to justify the possibility of commenting. We don't even need to propose some supernatural being like the Anima Mundi. There are even purely mechanical explanations of how divination can work to offer useful comments on the present; a number of creativity gurus recommend, for example, seeding new ideas with random input. On the other side, foretelling isn't limited to people who believe in magic. Weather forecasting isn't the only place people try to predict the future by extrapolating from present patterns: economics, politics, and advertising all attempt to make predictions.

The question of free will often arises in company with the question of foretelling, perhaps because fortune-telling can imply a fixed future. Many books on divination, especially astrology, go out of their way to assure the reader that the future is not fixed and that forecasting is, in fact, *inaccurate*, in the sense that, once warned, the querent can change his or her behavior. Many astrologers believe, for example, that when Neptune and Uranus come into conjunction, there are upheavals in the nature of community and belonging. The way those upheavals manifest, however, is shaped by the current situation. In the 1820s, for instance, a large number of countries broke away from their imperial governments, becoming independent. In 1990s, the next time these two planets came into conjunction, we saw the rise of the Internet uniting the world into a large information community. The details of these events were not fixed, but the conditions were suitable for their arising.

Many diviners believe that foretelling is more like forecasting—extrapolating the future from current patterns. This view of divination helps to explain why it's relatively tricky to predict the winner of a horse race. After all, no consciousness on earth really knows how the race will turn out, unless cheating is involved. The Anima Mundi is not omniscient: like us, she is situated in time, and she knows only what she knows, which is much more than any given human consciousness, but much less than everything. She might be able to take this horse's sore tendon, that jockey's new diet, and the thoughts of the surface of the track itself all into account and predict a winner—but it'd be a guess, albeit one with more information than you might have at the track.

Being a consciousness herself, the Anima Mundi is not a slave. When Croesus was debating whether or not to go to war with Cyrus, the king of the Persians, he consulted the Delphic oracle of Apollo. Now, whether the utterance came from Apollo or from the Anima Mundi is an academic question, but the nature of the response illustrates that answers are not devoid of personality. The oracle informed him, in clear and unambiguous terms, "If Croesus goes to war with Cyrus, he will destroy a mighty kingdom." Croesus rejoiced, went to war with Cyrus—and lost so spectacularly, and put such a strain on his financial and other resources, that he lost his kingdom. The oracle's forecasting was correct, just not what Croesus wanted to hear. A cynic could point out that this forecasting could be correct no matter what happened, but that's not true. If Croesus intended, not to destroy Cyrus' kingdom, but some nobler cause for going to war, he might hesitate at the prediction of this oracle. After all, he might say (as unlikely as it would be at this time), "I don't want to destroy the Persian kingdom; I just want to assure the freedom of its people from Cyrus's tyranny." But the oracle was telling him, "Because destruction is your goal, you will face destruction yourself."

Some people, among them A. E. Waite, regarded fortune-telling as frivolous, a parlor game for entertainment. Surely the Anima Mundi will not dance for our pleasure. But the story of Croesus also shows that divination faces some of the same issues: the Anima Mundi might say no. It is not wise to treat the underlying consciousness of the universe as a servant, whether at a party or in the temple of Delphi.

CHAPTER XIV

Synergy

Synergy is more than a business buzzword; it's an important concept in understanding any symbol system. Synergy is when two systems work together and the output exceeds the sum of the contribution of its individual parts.

Every symbol system relies on synergy for its meaning. Take, for example, the word "chair." If you try to define "chair," you will be forced to say something like "a kind of furniture on which one sits." Leaving aside a few inadequacies in that definition, you must now define "furniture" and "to sit." Doing so leaves us with even more terms, all of which must be defined. Finally we find ourselves having defined every single term with every other term, but without some of those terms to begin with, we're at a loss. That might be one reason we learn the initial vocabulary of a foreign language in reference to our native language, only later graduating to dictionaries in the second language.

The reliance on synergy also holds in cartomancy. If I define one card as covering a certain territory, I must recognize that I've defined other cards in the process. For example, in the vast and ill-defined stew of Lenormand meanings from diverse national traditions, you can find those who define 15–Bear as money, while you'll find others who suggest that 34–Fish is money, or 3–Ship. If we accept all these systems of meaning at the same time, we'll have three cards with the same meaning. But if you look closely at any one system, you'll see that each divides up the idea of "money" in different ways. For example, in the nascent American method of reading the Lenormand, I have seen 15–Bear to mean "cash flow," and 34–Fish to mean "general wealth and liquidity." Similarly, a traditional meaning of 35–Anchor is "job," but many American Lenormand readers, inspired by Sylvie Steinbach's system, prefer to use 14–Fox for "job" and 35–Anchor for "lifestyle." At one time, our job was a permanent thing that required only our stable attention. But now jobs are mobile and rely much more upon our wits than our sinews, even among those working class jobs like construction (anyone who thinks construction workers are just grunts has probably never been on a construction job).

This shift in meaning in the Lenormand also shows that a symbol system is in a holistic synergy with the culture itself. This synergy makes sense because what is a culture but a collection of symbols? So it stands to reason that we would need to divide up our culture in new ways to fit the old Lenormand.

Similarly, with the tarot, we have taken the twenty-two major arcana cards and defined their sequence as a story that can fit our lives. The archetypes of these cards have been abstracted as a sequence of stages of development, each of which gains its meaning from not just the cards before and after it but all the cards in the deck. We can define, for example, the Empress as "the love you experience in a nurturing bond, as with one's mother." But doing so means that we must define the Lovers as a different stage: the exteriorization of self-love to another.

The earliest tarot decks we can find probably didn't conceptualize the major arcana as a story in this way. I conclude this by the fact that they often didn't have the same ordering, for one thing. Moreover, some early decks contained cards that represented important ideas in the culture—the seven virtues, for example—but didn't sequence them as a stage of development. The "Fool's Journey" conceptualization of the tarot is a late addition. It's a useful late addition, however, because it recognizes the fundamental truth that each card in the tarot, like any part of a symbol system, has meaning only in relationship to the other symbols in that system, the other cards in the deck. A story is one of the easiest, most primal ways of organizing information and of showing those relationships between symbols.

Where the tarot is a story, a narrative, the Lenormand is like a map. Each of the symbols is a border surrounding some space on that map, defining possible meanings. We can classify the Lenormand cards and the ways they organize this space: some cards refer to people, some to money, some to love, some to psychological states, and some to objects. But each card stakes out a piece of the map for itself. The borders between these spaces are fuzzy, as they are in every symbol system. But at the same time, the meaning of one card does not encroach upon another. Both 36–Cross and 23–Mice are neighbors on that map of meaning. They can both indicate a state of worry, but they are different kinds of worry. 36–Cross is heavy and burdensome. 23–Mice is nervous and scurrying.

The overlap between symbols in the Lenormand is what programmers would call both a bug and a feature. If we want a chart of the universe, we would be better off with the tarot. If we try to map it in Lenormand terms, we'll find that our universe looks a lot like the daily concerns and hopes of a bourgeois eighteenth-century French woman. As I've said before, we are all a lot closer to bourgeois eighteenth-century French women than we are to Renaissance scholar-monks, who wrote the allegories the tarot images are based on. So, while the tarot might be a useful map of the universe, it isn't as likely to tell us about day-to-day things (yes, one can read the minor arcana for that, but even then—the divisions between cards are so neat, so tidy, it's hard not to read each of them, again, as a narrative in their elemental domain).

Can we read our lives as a particular episode in the grand archetypal narrative of the universe? We can, and it is useful to do so. But we are also ordinary people with ordinary concerns. If the tarot is a calligraphy pen, a Petit Lenormand (or a deck of playing cards, or any number of other cartomancy systems) is a ballpoint. A calligraphy pen is useful for some kinds of detailed, careful work; a ballpoint is a little more appropriate for day-to-day tasks. Few people, even calligraphers, write only with calligraphy pens.

It would be easy, even tempting, to claim that the concerns of the tarot—those big sweeping archetypal events—are more important than the day-to-day events spoken of in the Lenormand. Surely, the nurturing power of nature (the Empress) is more meaningful than the love and affection spoken of in 24–Heart. But what is 24–Heart but a manifestation, a cross-section, of that great story into the narrower dimensions of our lives?

And the Lenormand cards are also archetypes: the ring is 25–Ring, an archetype of union and agreement that transcends any given ring. To say that the Lenormand does not offer us archetypes of reality is false; it offers archetypes from the perspective of a person living an ordinary life. The tarot sees these archetypes through a magic mirror; the Lenormand, through the mirror over our bathroom sink.

If this is the case, why not combine the two and use both tools to give a more complete picture of a situation? Then we could create meaning not just from the synergy between the symbols in a single deck, but we can also create synergy between the two systems to provide even more meaning.

Let's imagine that we have a querent who is wondering about her relationship with her daughter, who is sixteen and whose friends the mother does not trust. We ask, "What does the querent need to know about her relationship with her daughter?"

We draw a tarot card, Temperance. It appears that the archetypal situation involves opposites that can become unified if tempered artfully. The querent suggest that perhaps this is her and her daughter, and that she lacks the art to temper the two: she cannot understand her daughter, and her daughter seems increasingly distant from her mother.

We ask, then, how this temperance might work out in the querent's daily life. We draw three Lenormand cards, charging the middle position with the querent. We draw 31–Sun, 5–Tree (in the place
of the querent), and 29–Lady. Interestingly, we would normally associate Lady with the querent, so we may decide that she and Tree go
together: she can be a force for health in her family. What about 31–
Sun? I ask the querent what she thinks.

"The sun is light, I suppose, and maybe part of the problem is I
haven't been really sharing with my daughter."

"What does that have to do with light in your mind?"

"Well, I mean, I could shine light on my life, couldn't I? And
maybe if I told her more about me, and less about rules and such,
she'd be more willing to share. It goes both ways."

I point to Temperance.

"Yes, like that. I've been trying to pour her into a cup without
realizing that I have to pour myself out too."

"What about the Tree card. I see that as important."

"I do too," the querent says. "You say it can mean health or family,
and I guess that makes sense. I see a tree in the background there in
the Temperance card, and I guess young trees need care too. She's like
a young tree, standing alone. No wonder she's trying to get friends
around her. That's just natural, I suppose, when you feel vulnerable
like that tree."

"Is that tree the only thing that's vulnerable?"

She looks at 29–Lady. "No. I am too. That card's me, right?"

"Usually it's the querent, when the querent's a woman. If it were
your daughter, I'd expect 13–Child instead."

"So it rests with me?"

"It would seem so."

To read this way, it helps to be aware not just of the meaning of
the cards but their images. As discussed earlier, many of the images
on the Lenormand appear in the tarot. It also helps to use the tarot
to narrow the meaning of the Lenormand. Is 14–Fox work, or cleverness? If the tarot card that accompanies it is the Fool, it's probably the
cleverness of the trickster. If it's the Magician, it might be the sort of

skills that apply to work. And if it's Strength, it's probably work—and hard work at that.

One tarot card is broad enough to shine light on several cards in the Lenormand deck. I've already described a 1:3 reading above, in which, after each of the Lenormand cards, we come back to the tarot. But we can also create different readings. For example, a layout I've invented that I call the shamrock reading can give an overview on a whole situation.

Lay four tarot cards, their bases together. The top card represents the intellectual or theoretical elements of the situation. The bottom card represents the emotional and unconscious elements of the situation. The card to the left is the practical and physical considerations. The card to the right is the energy that drives the situation: its origin and motivation.

Now, for each of the four tarot cards, lay out a pair of Lenormand cards. Consider the first of those cards to be the topic, and the second to be the comment. So, for example, I wish to know about a friend I haven't seen in some time. I lay out the cards as follows.

The intellectual situation is one of moving forward and overcoming. 12–Birds tells me that he is engaging in a lot of talk with official people: I know he wishes to get into a certain school. The indication seems to be that a lot of his mental power is bent on that task, and that it's going well.

Emotionally, I see that he's involved in a relationship. It's a long-distance one, but serious enough for it to affect his life strongly. Perhaps he might even move, or she might.

The Lovers tells me that in practical terms he must make a decision, one that involves a lot of hard work and independent thought. That would make sense: the school he is trying to go to will require a lot of him.

Finally, the force that drives him lately is the Magician. He happens to be one, so this set of skills and all of these life changes are probably in accordance with his will. 22–Crossroads tell me that he must make a decision soon, and clouds mark the uncertainty of the results of that decision. But the Magician seems to assure me that he'll juggle the situation appropriately and make a choice, even through the uncertainty. And that choice will, as the Chariot promises, get him where he wants to go.

After this reading, I had the opportunity to have dinner with my friend while attending a conference near his home city. As it turns out, he was indeed working to become accepted at a particular seminary, a decision he did not take lightly and was prompted to by carefully considered magical insight and deliberation. He also mentioned that he had met a woman who shared many of his interests, but that she lived in a different city and so they were waiting to see what the results of his application might be before making any rash decisions.

In an earlier chapter, I described a tarot procedure involving counting from particular tarot cards. We can combine this procedure with the Lenormand, laying out cards on top of the tarot cards to further refine their meaning as we count. Doing so is a dynamic process, almost as if we are divining the meaning of the tarot cards with the Lenormand cards. When we do so, we need to keep an eye on how the diverse symbol systems interact, not just on the level of what the cards mean, but also on the level of their graphic emblems. Here is where we can apply our discussion of the echoing of Lenormand symbols within the tarot: Lenormand cards that contain an image echoed in a tarot card take on added significance and also call our attention to that portion of the card.

For example, let's return to my reading about finances earlier.

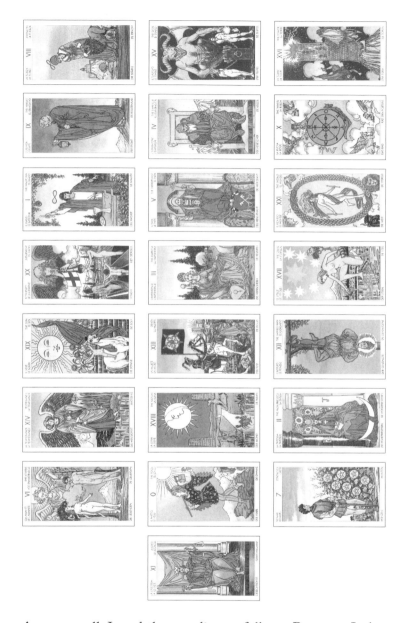

As you recall, I read the past line as follows. But now, I place a Lenormand card at each location.

The Lovers
(count 12 to ...)

Some choices I have made ...

The Magician
(count 7 to ...)

. . . involving education . . .

Judgement
(count 3 to ...)

. . . and a change in
lifestyle ... (viz., I was in college
a very, very long time)

Hermit
(count 12 to ...)

. . . and a career in teaching and
writing ...

Sun
(count 7 to ...)

. . . have proven beneficial ...

Temperance
(count 12 to ...)

. . . and wisely balanced.

The Hermit, so since this is a repeat, we stop.

Here we see the Lenormand giving the day-to-day interpretation of the error. Specifically, it says I was to go on a trip, but was weighed down (Anchor and Mountain). I'm fortunate to have the career I do, however, because it means that there is some hope (Stars and the tarot card the Sun). I might look to a friend skilled in money for advice.

The Fool (count 3 to …)	Jumping in without double-checking …

Death (count 12 to …)	… has led to a loss due to confusion (the adjacent Moon card indicates this).

The Devil (count 12 to …)	There's no way out of this mistake …

The Empress (count 7 to …)	… but overall, there's still growth. Don't panic (from the adjacent Hierophant).

Death, again, so since that's a repeat, we stop.

The foolish error was certainly painful. 11–Whip reminds me a bit visually of the Fool's bundle, which makes me think what he might have in it. Some solution to the problem, perhaps? The loss represented by Death is a nibble, rather than a full bite. It's mice chewing away at grain, potentially destructive but not as bad as it could be. The Devil combined with 8–Coffin, however, describe the emotional content of the error, however, quite well. The Empress promises growth, and 14–Fox counsels cleverness. Don't get trapped in the box of 8–Coffin or the chains of the Devil: think like a cunning fox. 23–Mice also reminds me that the Empress has grain at her feet: they didn't get it all.

The Chariot
(count 12 to …)

My car …

The World
(count 7 to …)

… can be brought full circle …

The Star
(count 12 to …)

… and offer some freedom and hope.

The Chariot, which is a repeat, so we stop.

One of the problems with using actual readings for examples is that they often look contrived. Here we have a pleasant outcome: 34–Fish promises independence and freedom, similar to the Chariot (and if you'll recall, the Chariot is associated with Cancer, certainly a sign friendly to 34–Fish). 9–Flowers promises a gift, and 15–Bear and the Star counsel hope for increased cash flow. The tarot card XVI–The Star of course points upward again to 16–Stars, the Sun in the past: what success was had in the past will be had in the future as well. It's almost too perfect, but I promise, I'm just reporting the cards as they fell.

Synergistic reading spurs intuition because it relies on it so heavily to integrate and reconcile the different symbol systems. It also requires and helps develop mental flexibility and symbolic thinking. It can be particularly powerful with collaborative approaches to reading. The most valuable feature of synergistic reading, however, is in my opinion the way in which it pulls us back from minutia into the big picture. By moving back and forth from one type of cartomancy to another in the same reading, we're forced to focus in on the details, then out to the big picture, several times. It's hard to define the sense of completeness and confidence that this procedure gives a reading, so I recommend trying it yourself.

CHAPTER XV

DIY

Every culture has its own means of divination, all of them different. And even different practitioners may regard symbols differently. For example, there's a long tradition of reading regular playing cards—not the tarot and not the Lenormand—and applying meanings to suits, numbers, or combinations thereof. This reading of playing cards is probably what Mlle. Lenormand herself did. Among those who read playing cards, it's not uncommon to find diverse meanings for particular cards. In the system I learned and employ, the Seven of Hearts means "emotional difficulty." Just glancing around the web at other meanings, I see that for some it means broken promises, for others platonic love, for others yet a female friend. Surely, then, the skeptic might scoff, there can be nothing to reading the cards, or everyone would agree on the meaning of individual cards.

The fallacious nature of this skeptical argument becomes clear when applied to other means of communication. For example, it's important if you're going to study Spanish to realize that *embarazada* does not mean "embarrassed." It may look similar, but assuming that a word means the same thing in Spanish as it does in English is likely to leave you embarrassed indeed (although probably not *embarazada*).

From this difference in meaning, we cannot conclude that no language really communicates. They all communicate, about equally well, because the meanings are arbitrarily applied to words, not by any conscious effort, but by unconscious agreement among speakers. And this agreement may change over time. The Spanish word *carpeta* means "folder," but in the southern parts of the United States, I understand that it has begun meaning "carpet" because of the similarity of those two words and a sort of unspoken and unconscious agreement to modify the word and its meaning.

Every system of divination is, at its root, DIY or "do it yourself." Every diviner creates new meanings for the symbols of his or her system. At the same time, however, there must be some agreement with the Anima Mundi or those symbols will remain dead and useless. Just as each speaker of English develops his or her own personal way of speaking the language—what linguists call an idiolect—but cannot simply create new words or grammar without being badly misunderstood, each diviner creates his or her own variations of meaning but cannot simply decide what a symbol means without understanding it in relation to all other symbols in that system. We can consult the Anima Mundi's opinion on what symbols mean by appealing to tradition, not blindly but with an intuitive openness and willingness to listen.

Try an experiment. Take ten slips of paper, and write a number on each, from one to nine, and then zero. Mix them up in a hat or upside down on the table, and then try to get into a divinatory state and ask for your phone number. Pull out the numbers one at a time. Did you end up with your phone number? I suspect not. Why not? Because for any symbol system to be an effective system of divination, it needs to follow some basic principles.

The first principle of all divination systems, which I've come back to repeatedly in this book, is that it serves as a method for listening to the Anima Mundi. In our example above, we listened—so listening is clearly not enough. The problem with the divination system of numbers written on slips of paper rests in the second principle of divination systems.

All good divination systems consist of a network of associated symbols. In the earlier discussion of the tarot, for example, I illustrated how cards in combination take on more meanings than merely adding the cards together. The Prince of Cups is a dreamy, thoughtful, poetic and emotional young person with a tendency to become distracted and start but not finish many projects. The Three of Swords is sorrow. Put them together and you don't simply have a young, poetic man. who is sad—you have a commentary on the cause of the sorrow. Perhaps the sadness evolves from this tendency to dream bigger than one's power to achieve. And if you add a third card to the mix, say the Nine of Cups, suddenly the entire meaning of the whole changes. Now, we see this sorrow is temporary because of unexpected good fortune fulfilling the wish of the young man represented. Now think of your phone number divination deck: the nature of the three in a phone number does not change when followed by the two. The symbols of the ten digits are part of a system, but not an associational system. The only association between the symbols of the digits and their places is whether they're to be multiplied by ten, a hundred, or a thousand, and so on—and even this is missing in a phone number.

So therefore, the second principle is that a divination system consists of a network of associated symbols. By "associated" I mean that the symbols signify their meaning in association with each other. They are not isolated but form a community of symbolic meaning. In this community, symbols (for example, words) are not defined in isolation as in a dictionary, but defined in their relationships to each other. These networks can become extremely complex, and to have "knowledge" of a topic is to understand, intuitively or otherwise, the network of meanings that defines the relationships between its parts. A divination system, to be effective, apparently must have a certain level of associational complexity. In our deck, the network of meaning is not complex: each node (card) is simply one of a set of arbitrarily defined numbers.

The third principle of a good divination system arises out of the second. A good divination system does not reveal facts but meanings. A fact in isolation is not meaningful because it does not have a relationship with other vertices in a semantic network. Your phone number is a fact. The Anima Mundi, however, is a consciousness dwelling completely in meaning; for her, your phone number is nearly invisible. Just as we are unconscious of the individual muscle fibers moving in our legs as we walk, so she is unconscious of the facts that, together, make up meaning. If we wish to divine a phone number, we need to imbue it with meaning. How we might do this is beyond my imagination, but other such facts—the locations of missing objects, for example—becomes easy to divine when the diviner focuses on the meaning of the object, rather than seeing it as a lifeless material object. The more sensory and emotional connection we can have with a thing, the more it means.

Our number deck fails as a divination system again, because we have no sensory experience of numbers themselves. We have experience with physical objects reflecting the properties of the numbers: we have experience of "two pens" and "two cupcakes" and "two books" but not of "two." And you cannot substitute the sensory and emotional meaning of "two cupcakes" for that of "two pens." But a phone number doesn't even have the physicality of that association. The area code 630 does not represent six hundred thirty of anything: it's just an arbitrary code.

Finally, our number deck fails because of the fourth principle of a good divination system: completeness. For a divination system to operate well, it must represent a microcosm of the Anima Mundi's consciousness. It must serve as a psychological map of her awareness, which is the entire universe. This map can be large-grained, and such a map might be more useful than an exact one—after all, a full-sized map of a place can never exist, without destroying the place it maps. Lon Milo DuQuette calls this quality of a divination system "perfection,"[29] which is an apt description. The word "perfect" actually comes from a Latin root meaning "complete." A tarot deck is

---

29. Lon Milo DuQuette, *The Book of Ordinary Oracles* (Boston: Weiser, 2005), 26-27.

"perfect" in this sense, because it divides up and maps the entirety of experience in more-or-less accurate proportions.

Sometimes one comes across a divination system, usually sold in boxed sets, that is made up by an individual or channeled from some supposedly spiritual source. Some of these fortune-telling decks are excellent, but some of them are "imperfect." They sometimes have, for example, no indication of anything negative that could ever happen to anyone. Such a deck might be pretty and comforting, but probably is not terribly accurate. If you don't give the Anima Mundi a way to say "watch out!" how will she warn you about the sharks?

So is our number deck useless? Not entirely. If we can create significance for these numbers, we can begin to create our own divination deck. We might not be able to use it to divine phone numbers (after all, they are facts and not meaning, and therefore not really what divination is for, just as you can't smelt iron in a microwave). But we can use it for other purposes. If you take your ten numbers and begin to imagine what they could mean, what events they might represent, you've taken a few steps toward creating a divination system.

In defining these symbolic meanings, keep in mind that you're dividing up the entire universe into ten chunks, so you need to be large-grained in your approach. You want big trends, not details. Let's imagine that you decide, reasonably enough, that one indicates beginnings, two indicates partnerships or exchanges, and three indicates blessings, and so on. You might decide differently: three might indicate growth because a mother and a father create new life, or it might represent danger because a three-sided figure cannot stand stably on its point. Whatever seems most reasonable to you will work if you're consistent. Now you have a deck suitable for marking large-scale trends and relationships in your life.

But it's not very precise. It is a map with too few details, like one that mentions the existence of London and New York but little else between. Handy if you're trying to find London from New York, not so handy if you're trying to find Alsip, IL, from Dubuque, IA. You draw, say "one" and ask, "Well, great, beginnings—but what's beginning?" What we have here is a list of symbolic relationships between ideas, but not the ideas themselves. Yet we cannot create a divination system that includes every possible idea in the universe, or even in our experience of the universe. Such a system would rapidly become cumbersome indeed, like a map of California the size of the state itself.

But we can add some general domains of human experience to the deck, to define our terms a bit. We could, for example, decide that the main interactions that people undertake involve emotional situations, represented by hearts; work, represented by sticks or staves; conflict, represented by swords (after all, we want to include all experiences, not just the good ones); and material possessions, represented by a precious stone, like a diamond. Now we have a deck with ten pips and four suits. We have the pips of playing cards without the court cards.

We can take these cards and write a general meaning on each card, a short title that expresses the nature of each card. For example, the Ace of Spades is the beginning of strife. That makes sense. Maybe we've decided that fours are stability, so the Four of Diamonds is financial stability. If threes are growth then the Three of Clubs is increased work. What we have now is a traditional fortune-telling deck, built from the ground up rather than memorized out of a book. And we can see, therefore, why the meanings might differ from reader to reader—my Six of Clubs is probably not your Six of Clubs.

We're not bound by these numbers, the key of ten and the key of four. Any of the keys can be used to create a system of more or less complexity. These numeric keys survive as well as they do inasmuch as they represent a map of human experience, so any of them may be used to create meaning. Relationships between them can be multiplicative, as we've done here with the deck of cards, or additive, as the twenty-two cards of the major arcana are added to the deck of the fifty-six minor arcana. We could, for example, create a system that involved the three aspects of cardinal, fixed, and mutable, and the seven planets. If we multiply them, we'd end up with twenty-one tokens, a manageable number. Then we figure out how the combinations ring changes upon the symbols: fixed Venus is emotional stability; cardinal Venus may be the beginning of a relationship. Or we could ring the changes of each planet through the four elements: fire of Venus may be passion; water of Mars may be anger.

Or we could add the keys instead of multiplying them: we could take the twelve archetypes of the signs and create cards for each, then add to that cards for each of the elements. We could also combine methods, as the tarot does, and create one set of cards with multiplicative relationships and add to it another set of symbols: the planets through the elements, for example, and then the twelve signs on top of that to create a deck of seven times four plus twelve. And the possibilities for permutation are nearly endless. For example, geomancy and I Ching both permute in binary, zero, or one. In geomancy, there are four binary digits, represented by one dot or two in each of four lines to create sixteen figures. In I Ching, there are six lines, called a "hexagram," each with a broken or whole line, to create sixty-four figures. In both cases, we get the same sort of multiplicative process described earlier.

So many different divination systems make use of this multiplicative approach because it serves two purposes: first, it creates a complete system by covering all possible permutations of two different symbol systems or keys. Second, it assures relationships between symbols in at least two directions: it acts as a center for the arising of a web of meaning. In geomancy, for example, certain characters are opposites of other characters, and others are reversals of those characters, so each symbol has a relationship with, often, two other characters. And anyone who has worked with the I Ching more than simply looking up the commentary on each hexagram realizes that each hexagram is composed of two trigrams, one on top of the other, and two inner trigrams, interlocked in the middle of the figure, which themselves create a hexagram.

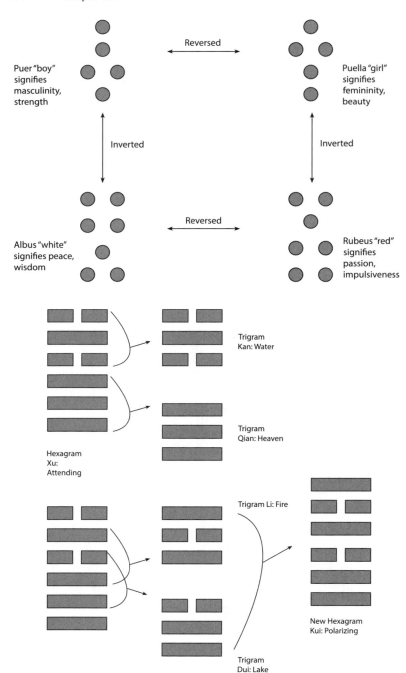

Puer "boy" signifies masculinity, strength

Puella "girl" signifies femininity, beauty

Reversed

Inverted

Inverted

Albus "white" signifies peace, wisdom

Rubeus "red" signifies passion, impulsiveness

Reversed

Trigram
Kan: Water

Trigram
Qian: Heaven

Hexagram
Xu:
Attending

Trigram Li: Fire

Trigram
Dui: Lake

New Hexagram
Kui: Polarizing

Some divination systems, however, simply include a list of archetypes and trusts in the tradition to assure both completion and relationships between them. I've used cards marked for each of the twelve Olympian gods, for example, to some good effect, because each card invokes a series of stories. For example, if I lay out Aphrodite next to Ares, I can tell the story of their relationship, and if Hephaestos comes up, then I can tell the story of how he caught them in a net for the gods to jeer at—a clear divinatory message of "whatever is being kept hidden will be uncovered by cleverness." The completion or perfection of this system relies on the reader's power of association and memory. The runes are one such system, in which each of the runes acts as a hyperlink to various stories, legends, and practices of the Norse people.

Often these latter systems, in which a series of notions or archetypes create the divinatory system, may be codified into a text-based divination system. In this case, the relationships between symbols exists in the stories themselves, and the symbols alone mean relatively little unless one knows the texts. In the I Ching, the hexagrams relate to each other through their component trigrams, but they also point to various texts with consistent characters, like "The Superior Man" and consistent symbolism, such as "crossing a great water." The Yoruba divination system, Ifa, uses symbols very similar to the geomantic symbols to point to a set of oral verses. The diviner and querent work together to apply the oral verses indicated by the fall of the shells to the querent's situation.

All truly useful divination systems will eventually situate their symbols into a narrative framework. If the symbols have no "story-meaning," then they're impossible to apply to life. For example, one can say that the rune Tiwaz means courage and success, but it's more useful to tell stories of Tyr and watch the querent's reaction. Similarly, the Fool in the tarot means beginnings, setting out, and so on—but you're better off recognizing that he is a character in a story. He's not simply the idea of setting out: he's a person setting out, with a bag on his shoulder (what's in the bag?) and a dog at his heels (is the dog helpful or harmful?) and a cliff before him (is he aware of it? Will he fall?). Each of these questions is a story hook that you can use to connect the reading to the querent's life situation.

In creating your own divination system, it helps to begin by recognizing the kind of stories you wish the system to tell. If you want a divination system to tell you specifically about one area of life, you can leave out some symbols, as long as you're complete in that domain. Similarly, if you want a divination system that can be used universally, like the tarot, you need to include every possible life event, to some degree, so that you can tell any story that arises.

Moreover, you need to recognize that stories are not single entities, but symbols strung together into meaningful patterns. A story is not mechanical. I remember when I was learning the tarot I picked up a fairly well-intentioned book with lots of good advice, but one of the things it suggested was that in a drawing for a yes/no question, an upright card was always yes and a reversed card was always no. Always in search of mechanical simplicity, I tested this technique and found it right—about 50 percent of the time. What I found more often was that the meaning of the card itself told the story that answered the question, and not always simply—because, in reality, there are no simple yes/no questions. There are stories that we tell ourselves about our lives.

In order to take advantage of the organic nature of these stories, it helps to have symbols that work together in combination. A. O. Spare, in a famous essay on cartomancy, suggests creating your own deck, assigning unambiguous but fairly broad meaning to each of the cards. The complexity comes from creating a story of the cards as they fall:

> It is the **combination** of certain cards that indicates the meanings of the more important events and episodes of life. For example: a combination of Spades - 'Nine,' 'Ten,' and 'Ace' - when so closely juxtaposed would mean death very soon and, in combination with cards meaning 'accident,' 'sickness,' 'hate,' would mean death by accident,

sickness, murder or suicide, and so on covering every possible event.[30]

If we can gloss over his characteristic grimness, we see that he goes on to suggest that the more cards necessary to create a meaningful combination, the more unlikely the event. Marriage might be indicated with two or three cards; marriage to—oh, say—the duke of Ostfriesland, however, might require more cards.

One advantage of sticking with the keys of four and ten mentioned earlier is that we already have pre-made cards with those numbers associated. We can use playing cards as a divination system right out of the box.

Methods of reading regular playing cards vary in terms of how much the suits and numbers mean. One way of creating a divination system is simply to apply an arbitrary meaning to every card. This seems to be what Spare is suggesting. The memory load of such a practice is high. But the advantages are that you can get every symbol you want, somewhere. He suggests writing them on the cards to aid memory.

We can also use our keys, as previously discussed, to create meanings. For example, we can decide that each of the digits from ace to ten represents part of a story. The ace is the beginning, the twos are the ally who aids us. Three is the desire that drives the plot. Four is the setting. Five is the obstacle that must be overcome. Six is the way through. Seven is the weapon we use. Eight is the plan. Nine is success. Ten is completion. Now, we can decide that each of the suits represents a domain of experience: hearts are emotion; spades are the mind; clubs are activity and work; diamonds are money. Now the Five of Clubs is an obstacle at work. The Two of Hearts is an ally in love: a friend. The Three of Diamonds is the desire for money. The Seven of Clubs is the tools of our trade. The Seven of Spades is our wits. The Nine of Hearts is success in love.

---

30. A. O. Spare, *The Zöetic Grimoire of Zos,* http://hermetic.com/spare/grimoire_of_zos.html.

204 • *Chapter XV*

Another system, the Hedgewytch system, described on an unfortunately now defunct website, gave each digit a meaning based partially upon the appearance and arrangement of the pips. Ones are beginnings. Twos are partnerships and exchanges. Three is growth. Four is stability. Five is the body and its accoutrements. Six is the path. Seven is an obstacle. Eight is the mind. Nine is success. Ten is completion. Then the suits are divided by color: red is the pleasant domains of love (hearts) and money (diamonds). Black is the less pleasant domains of work (clubs) and trouble (spades). Now we can see that Three of Spades is an increase in worry; Two of Diamonds is a monetary partnership.

The court cards, in most systems of cartomancy, often represent people, with jacks being juveniles, queens being women, and kings being men. So the King of Spades might be a man who uses his wits: a lawyer or judge. A Jack of Diamonds might be a young man who has just begin to gather "goods"—a student, perhaps. Traditionally the court cards are also given domains of their own: jacks are often, across systems, associated with messages. So the Jack of Hearts is a message about love. The Hedgewytch system associates queens with "truth" and kings with "power," so the Queen of Spades is an unpleasant truth; the King of Diamonds, the power of wealth.

The Hedgewytch system in full is complex; it is a pity that the site that described it has disappeared. Hopefully, the author of the system will publish it elsewhere.

But we can create our own, just as easily. The benefit of using playing cards is that they are, unlike the tarot and unlike the Petit Lenormand, nearly blank. We can project whatever symbolism, whatever image, we have on them. That's also the source of their intimidation. They require us to map out a universe before we shuffle. Some readers of the tarot prefer unillustrated pip cards—minor arcana without images—for just this reason: they can project an interpretive framework on them themselves rather than having it imposed by the artist.

Even if we don't create our own divination systems, we all do create the stories that the cards or runes or I Ching tell us. We create the combinations and links between symbols that create meaning from the system, and my combinations differ from yours, because the stories I habitually tell and experience also differ from yours. Some books misunderstand this process of story-telling, and list long lists of combinations that one is, presumably, to memorize. However, they're best used as examples for the basic idea, and not as mechanical meanings imposed upon the story. The story imposes meaning on the cards; the cards do not impose meaning on the story.

Any "perfect" or complete system will lend itself to story-telling, and story-telling lends itself to divination because stories are predictable. Once you understand their structure, it's difficult to be surprised. One of the jokes among those who study literature is that movies are ruined for them forever: there are only a few limited plots, recycled again and again, and once you learn them, movies become predictable. Of course, we still watch movies, because although we know how the movie will end, we don't know for sure how the movie will get there. Divining the future lets us see how the plot we've chosen to live out is likely to end, but that doesn't rob us of the interest of living it. And unlike characters in a movie, we can choose our plots, change our future, and divination can help us do that. Do-it-yourself divination isn't just creating a new system of cards or runes, or constructing and learning new ways to combine the symbols of your favorite system: it's also learning how to write the story you live yourself. Divination is a language that works in both directions.

CHAPTER XVI

Divination and Magic

A divination system is a set of symbols that not only describes experience but can shape it. A divination shapes experience into a narrative, a story that we can tell ourselves or our querent. Sometimes, this story isn't the story we want to act out, and that's when we need more active options.

We can revise the story we live in with the same symbols we use to read it. The symbols the Anima Mundi uses to communicate with us may also be used to communicate with her. When she helps us read our story, we can also help tell our story back to her. In other words, we collaborate with the universe in creating our stories.

Foresight

Not everything can be altered, if for no other reason than that we don't really want to. Perhaps you notice in a reading that your business prospects look good but your prospects in romance seem less good. You could try to fix that, giving yourself equal success in both, and you may be successful. But if you're the sort of person who would really rather spend extra time at the office, do you really want good prospects in love? Perhaps not, if they would distract you from your real interests. Magic requires that you learn what you really want, and divination can help with that.

You also may not want to modify your reading because you're unsure of the ultimate results. I once interviewed for a job in another city. It paid well, the people seemed nice, and it promised lots of time to write. It wouldn't be challenging, but it would be pleasant. I'd have to relocate, but I was single at the time and would have welcomed a change in scenery. I did a reading on whether I'd get the job after the second interview and the cards unambiguously said, "No, you're not getting the job." This reading didn't match my experience. I nailed the interviews and felt confident.

On the flight back, I considered whether or not to do magic to get the job, just to make sure. I saw the lights of Chicago spread out under me as we approached O'Hare, and I started thinking about the deep-dish pizza I could get at the airport before I drove home. I really wanted the job. But I also realized that I liked the city I lived in and didn't mind sticking around it longer.

I chose, instead, to do magic for a more general aim: to get a position that suited me in the Chicago area. The results were spectacular, but that's another story, and I often think that if I had saddled myself with that other job, appealing as it was, I wouldn't have the extremely pleasant (knock on wood) life I have now.

A lot of magicians perform divinations before doing any act of practical magic to prevent unforeseen side effects. The usual reason given is the monkey's-paw syndrome. "The Monkey's Paw" is a short story by W. W. Jacobs.[31] In it, a family receives a dried monkey's paw from a family friend, who claims to have gotten it from a holy man in India. It can grant three wishes, but they always turn out badly. The family wishes for money, then loses their son in a terrible accident and gets paid by the insurance company. In sorrow, the mother wishes for the return of her son, and they hear shuffling footsteps outside the

---

31. W. W. Jacobs, "The Monkey's Paw" *Gaslight* (orig. 1902) http://gaslight .mtroyal.ca/mnkyspaw.htm.

door. Finally, realizing that his son has returned as a monster, the father wishes for his son to be back in the grave. The moral of the story is that fate rules our lives, and we should not wish for it to be different.

I'm not so convinced that the Anima Mundi is either so literal-minded or so malicious. One can use magic to cause harm, and one can accidentally cause harm through miscommunication, but I don't think it's worthwhile to regard the Anima Mundi as a monkey's paw, nor is the moral of that story particularly apt for those of us who practice magic. After all, we change fate all the time: passive acceptance of chance is hardly a magical attitude. On the other hand, active acceptance of a situation is sometimes required. By active acceptance, I mean recognizing that sometimes we endure hardship in order to meet a larger good later. I just got back from my morning jog, and let me tell you, I'd have rather sat on the couch and eaten strawberries while watching reruns. But thirty minutes of panting and sweating is worth it if it improves my health and gives me more time to enjoy my life. Also, some hardships are unassailable. Sometimes bad things happen and we can't do anything about them but learn to accept them. Magic will not solve all problems any more than any other technology can.

I think a preliminary divination is useful, however, because we can't always know whether or not a greater good is in the offing. Staying in Chicago has influenced my life for the better in a way I couldn't have predicted before. If I had willy-nilly forced myself into a position I was not suited for, I might have found myself much less happy. It's useful to perform a divination not just before the magical ritual, but as part of it, to see what areas are likely to succumb to force and which are likely to remain implacable.

Practical Magic

But the role of cartomancy in magic doesn't have to stop at divination alone. We can use the cards as a symbol system in their own right. There's a long tradition of this practice in the tarot. For example, Donald Michael Kraig describes using the tarot in conjunction with the

Qabalah as a tool not only for introspection but actual internal and external change.[32] And Donald Tyson describes an entire ceremonial system working with nothing but the images of the tarot; this system, complete in its own right, could be an entire magical practice.[33]

As I've described elsewhere, I think of magic as a means of communicating with the underlying consciousness of reality itself through symbols. Seen in that light, divination is only magic going in the other direction. Magic and divination are two turns in a conversation, and we can use the same language the Anima Mundi uses to speak to us to talk back to her. We can ask questions, and we can also make statements. One of the advantages of using cartomantic symbols for magic is that one can carry them around easily; magic becomes portable. It doesn't take much practice before a cartomancer can call up the image in memory of a detailed figure on a card at a moment's notice. For this reason, many of my favorite techniques of cartomantic magic involve "street magic," or on-the-fly enchantment.

There are as many things one can do with the symbols of cartomancy as there are magical practices in general. Rather than trying to provide an exhaustive, and exhausting, list, I'll just mention some of the practices I have used.

The quantity of books on using the tarot in practical magic grows at a slow but steady rate. I highly recommend Donald Tyson's *Portable Magic*, and Donald Michael Kraig's *Tarot & Magic*. Some of the same techniques described in those books can be applied to the Lenormand. But the Lenormand particularly suits itself to a folk-magic approach, rather than the formal magic described in Tyson's and Kraig's books.

One of the great advantages of the Lenormand is that the decks are so inexpensive; you can get a classical Piatnik for twelve dollars. While it's kind of hard to carry around tarot cards as talismans, you can carry around Lenormand cards and not worry about destroying

---

32. Donald Michael Kraig, *Tarot & Magic* (St. Paul, MN: Llewellyn, 2003).

33. Donald Tyson *Portable Magic: Tarot Is the Only Tool You Need* (Woodbury, MN: Llewellyn, 2006).

them, because they're easily replaced. Moreover, Lenormand cards are much smaller than tarot, which makes them convenient talismans.

And you can always simply draw the relevant images on a piece of parchment or paper, perhaps as part of a more formal talisman. A talisman is a written or drawn object, or sometimes a natural object, regarded as having some mystical power, usually protective or attractive. For example, there are folk-magic talismans to prevent harm while traveling, or to win at gambling, and so on. Many talismans are simply written on a piece of paper, either as a complex traditional seal or a more freeform collection of symbols. In Western magic, particularly that influenced by Hermeticism, the talisman must be activated in some way. Often this involves a ritual designed to create life in it the object. Folk-magic traditions are simpler: the talisman is simply treated as if it's alive: in Hoodoo, it might be anointed with particular substances, or "fed" in some way. In other folk-magic traditions, the symbol itself is already regarded as alive or powerful.

If you wished to create a ritual to enliven a Lenormand card, you could apply the same procedure you use to create a signifier when reading the cards. For example, say you wished to use 4–House to protect your home. You might draw the figure in an inconspicuous place, then imagine it becoming the signifier of your home while you surround it with symbols of protection. In this way, the Lenormand can be used as a library of symbols to represent any particular need or goal.

We can also use the Lenormand in more direct folk magic, such as the practice of candle magic or setting lights. The Lenormand are suited to setting lights. Here's a simple spell to give you a notion of how it works, and you can elaborate on it yourself if so inclined.

1. You need only a candle and a Lenormand deck.

2. You need to choose three cards. The first is your signifier, so that's easy. The second and third represent your desire. Select these as a combination, so that the first represents your situation and the second the modification you wish to apply. So, for example, if you are blocked creatively, you might choose

21–Mountain to represent the block and 16–Star to represent overcoming the block and being more creative.

3. In selecting a candle, choose one that is of an appropriate color; several tables of correspondence between color and desire exist, but you can if you wish just follow common sense. Alternately, you can choose a candle related to a relevant saint, if you have them available in your location and wish to work with saints. I would choose a yellow candle to represent creativity; other people may prefer other colors to represent the same idea.

4. Begin by laying out the cards with the signifier at the top, the situation card to the left bottom, and the result to the bottom right. Place the candle in the middle of the triangle thus formed. Touch the signifier, then the situation. Feel the weight of the situation on your shoulders, then move your finger to the result and imagine the change occurring. Visualize some concrete sign of the change; I might see myself working again after a creative block. Try to imagine it as vividly as possible, and while holding it in your mind, light the candle.

5. Let the candle burn out. If you cannot do so (and it really isn't safe to leave a candle unattended) you can extinguish it by smothering or pinching and relight it later. When you do relight it, as counterintuitive as it sounds, try not to visualize the effect you want. Focus intently on the candle instead, and the sensory experience of relighting it. Try not to think again about your goal consciously. Burn the whole candle for the spell, even after it seems to be working. This simple ritual can be elaborated as you like. For example, perhaps you want to add semiprecious gemstones on top of the cards, which you can carry in a gris-gris bag. Or you want to dress the candle with oil. Or you can put the cards on your altar and perform a rather more ceremonial ritual. You can draw the cards, or a stylized symbol of them, on a talisman. You can even invoke the figures on the cards in your imagination and ask them for advice on how to elaborate the ritual or make it more effective.

Revising a Reading

You can also mingle divination and magic. It's not uncommon in tarot practice for people to rearrange cards after doing a reading. I've had good luck simply rearranging the cards I get into a more favorable position. The same events occur, but by rearranging them I've repurposed them. After rearranging the cards, I contemplate the new spread, not with the intent to interpret it but with the intent to send it as a message back. I like to attain a miniature trance here, just by concentrating intently upon my signifier. Then, once I feel the imperceptible shift that indicates my message has been sent, I'll pick up and shuffle the cards, putting it out of my mind.

Sitting down to read the cards can itself be an act of practical, active magic rather than strictly receptive divination. When you sit down with the intent that the spread of the cards is a suggestion of what may happen, and you can and will modify it, you turn reading into practical magic. It's helpful in such readings to have a layout that keeps cards "in store," for you to manipulate during the reading. You can conceive of these cards as possible futures from which you will select as you read. A useful spread for that is as follows:

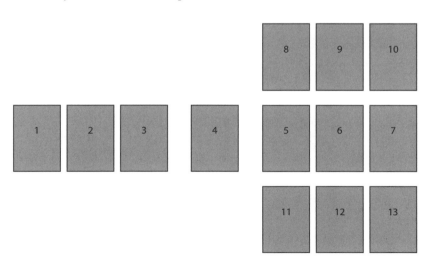

Charge place 4 with your signifier. Remember, that means project the image of your signifier on it mentally, but you don't have to dig the signifier out of the deck. Cards 1, 2, 3, all indicate the past. Read them in combination. If it matches the past as you know it, then you know you're on the right track. Card 4 is the current situation, or your current state of mind. Because it's in a place charged with the signifier, you should read it as though it were a personal state, not necessarily a universal one. In other words, 25–Ring might mean an agreement or contract with yourself, probably not a contract between two other people.

Cards 5, 6, 7 all indicate the current likely future. In other words, if you walk away from this spread, this is what will probably happen. Sometimes, you find that comes out rather nicely—in which case, you have no need to do magic.

Cards 8, 9, 10, and 11, 12, 13 all indicate alternate futures, ones that are less likely but within the realm of possibility. Read each of them as combinations, then consider if one of them seems better than what you currently have. If so, put them over cards 5, 6, and 7. Perhaps you like the future depicted in 8, 9, and 10 better. Pick them up and let them cover the current future.

As you do so, name the cards in turn and describe how you want the card to manifest. So, for example, I might want to replace something grotty, like 21–Mountain, 36–Cross, 6–Clouds with another possibility, such as 26–Book, 33–Key, 1–Rider. As I cover the first future with them, I explain what I want them to mean. I'm speaking aloud, not only to myself but to the Anima Mundi:

"I find the knowledge (lay down 26–Book) to a secret (lay down 33–Key) that will help me move forward (1–Rider)."

Take away the other possible future, and now repeat three times what you intend to happen, touching teach card in turn. When you finish doing so, contemplate only the images on the cards, driving from your mind any meaning behind them. Three more times, touch the cards while simply letting the symbols sink into your mind. Now, finishing that, do the same again, but this time imagine the symbols expanding from the cards outward to fill the entire universe.

Then, pick up all the cards and shuffle thoroughly. You may also wish to perform a banishing ritual, although since the cards have become your magical tools and the invoked forces themselves, shuffling is usually banishing enough.

Since you have two possibilities, you may choose from either. You may also rearrange the orders of cards as you see fit, and perhaps you don't want to replace every card in the future. The example above described a singularly dismal future; perhaps there is a silver lining in yours that you want to keep, but to emphasize. For example, maybe I don't much mind a delay, or even a heavy burden depicted by 36–Cross, but I really don't want to face confusion in the future. In that case, I might just replace 6–Clouds with 33–Key and do the same. I could even re-describe what I intend cards to mean: Instead of "delay," maybe I will say, "I will find the solitude to focus on spiritual pursuits" to describe 21–Mountain and 36–Cross.

I'll point out what is probably obvious to those who are inclined to magic: we can combine this spell-reading with the candle spell described earlier. The goal here is just to acquire a set of symbols to use in magic that are particularly well-suited to the task at hand. We could do the same procedure, if we liked, with the tarot or with another system of divination: runes, geomancy, tarot, or other oracle cards.

Like most topics in magic, the real way to explore this idea is to practice it. Experiment with using the cards for magic, and you'll learn more—and it'll be more relevant to your experience—than anything I could tell you in a book. Divination and magic based on it requires experimentation that fits your particular circumstances. One of the advantages of using cards like the tarot or the Lenormand for magic is that it strips us of our excuses. After all, it doesn't take an elaborate temple. I don't need to get out my special folding table. I don't have to gather my wand and other tools. I just need to shuffle and lay out the cards on any available surface (which does, usually, involve shifting some piles of books—but not putting on a robe). By the same token, we can do much more elaborate things if we like.

Scrying

One of my favorite techniques is one that requires just an armchair and some privacy. The Golden Dawn called it "scrying in the spirit vision," and despite the grandiose name it's actually simple. It's a bit like a nondirected fantasy. Jung described it as "active imagination," suggesting that it was a method of taking advantage of one's dream therapy in a more self-directed state. At the same time, it's been called "astral projection" or even an "out-of-body experience," although I don't particularly care for that term.

In the simplest terms, what it comes down to is eliciting an extremely vivid, directed, but autonomous daydream. *Daydream* isn't a strong enough word: perhaps "mental journey" might be more accurate.

For Jung, we begin with a dream which we revisit in a conscious state, nevertheless letting our unconscious create the environment and action of the dream. For example, perhaps I have a dream of going the store and not being able to buy anything because I forgot my wallet. I go back to that dream in my conscious state, and simply imagine myself standing in line again, realizing that I've lost my wallet. Then I let the dream continue, but this time I'm conscious of it. Perhaps my unconscious causes the teller to say something significant that helps me understand the tension that gave rise to the dream, or perhaps I notice that I'm buying stuff I don't need and the tension is released. Whatever occurs, it's an opportunity for the conscious mind to meet the unconscious mind on neutral territory, in which neither has absolute control.

What the practitioners of the Golden Dawn realized was that you don't need to use a dream: any symbol will do to crystallize such a vision. For example, they used elemental symbols, exploring worlds related to the five Hindu elements. Other magicians have used symbols like the runes. And Donald Michael Kraig describes ways of using the tarot.

We can also use the Lenormand. For example, if we choose to scry 9–Flowers, we can explore the esoteric power of beauty in our life. Similarly, we can explore and gain power over the slyness of 7–Snake.

A lot of stuff—I'll be polite and call it "stuff"—has been written about astral travel. Most of it makes the whole thing out to sound much more complicated than it really is. We are given, in at least some sources, dire warnings about deluding ourselves, or only exploring our own minds instead of the world at large. We're told that if the "ray" isn't concentrated enough it won't be able to pierce the sphere of sensation, and other such profound-sounding bits of claptrap. And on the other side, we get stern statements that if you do it in this way rather than that way, you're doing it wrong. Frankly, my attitude is, if you get results, you're doing it right.

In reality, whether you explore your own mind or the world outside it, you are exploring the mind of the Anima Mundi. Yes, you will eventually have the awareness that you are receiving information external to yourself. Inevitably, you will begin to understand the position of your own mind in that of the mind at large. But it begins with an activity children do instinctively: imagination.

How to Scry a Card

1. First, choose a card. You can do this by drawing a card after asking, "What do I need to work on" but you can also select a card by reasoning it out. For example, if I wish to work on worry, perhaps I could use 36–Cross. But maybe I want to start a bit softer, and get some control of my fears and concerns first by working through 24–Heart.

2. Begin by relaxing, perhaps by using the fourfold breath or any other method that works well for you. Falling asleep while scrying isn't a disaster, but it might be hard to remember what you experience if you do enter into a dreaming state in the middle of scrying.

3. Now imagine that you are standing up. You may begin by seeing yourself from the third person, as if watching a movie. Slowly build up detail, including your clothing, your facial expression, and so on. Jan Fries recommends starting in a misty

environment that slowly clears, allowing you to activate each astral sense in turn,[34] and this can be useful, but it's also useful to build up a location that you can remember clearly and easily: perhaps a childhood location or even an imaginary temple.

4. Once your body is ready, move your point of view into it. You may have some trouble keeping this up—your mental eye might roam back to the third person from time to time. That's okay: don't worry about it. Eventually, you will stay more or less within the viewpoint of the so-called astral body. It really doesn't matter to the efficacy of the practice as long as you can identify, at times, with the astral body. After all, we don't always see ourselves from within our bodies: we often construct a mental third-person image of ourselves in our minds.

5. Let the mist clear, or open your eyes, and see with as much detail as possible the environment in which you find yourself. Activate all your senses: sight, hearing, smell, and touch. I have a mental temple with an altar that I set my hand on; once I can feel the chisel marks on the stone, I know I'm ready.

6. Visualize a door of some kind with the relevant emblem on it. With the tarot, this requires a good memory for images. With the Lenormand, it requires merely that you can visualize a version of the central emblem for which the card is named. For 24–Heart, this is a heart. It doesn't have to be the specific image from any particular deck; a generic heart shape will do. I do like to visualize the number of the card as well, but this too is optional.

7. Once you have the door—or perhaps a curtain—open it and step through. Take note of your environment and begin to explore it. Remember the rule of fairy tales: everything is significant. At the same time, if you find yourself making stuff

---

34. Jan Fries, *Helrunar: A Manual of Rune Magick* (Oxford: Mandrake), 1993.

up, let go and let images and experiences arise, even if they don't make sense.

An Example of Scrying

For example, imagine I'm dealing with the issue of gaining power over my emotions. I select a card—24–Heart—and familiarize myself with its look. After relaxing and imagining myself entering into my imagined body in a temple space, I activate each of my senses and project the image of the card on a door in front of me.

I step into the card and immediately notice that I'm on a dirt path in a forest. A path begs to be followed, so I follow it. I hear animal sounds in the forest: small, benign, Midwestern sorts of animals, like the woods where I grew up. I see a spindly shape bounding between trees: a spirit? No, a deer. Although, I reflect, a deer could also be a spirit.

A flash of color through the trees reveals a cottage. I approach. It's a small stone hut, one room, with a thatch roof and a small door of rough, but thick, wood. I knock and there's a shuffle from within. An ancient woman opens the door.

I learned this technique in a tradition suspicious of—well, everything. So I test her by sending the image of a heart flying toward her. The heart disappears and, if anything, she looks older. If she were a deception, self or otherwise, she would have wavered, faded, or changed when confronted with the symbol of the realm. "Come in," she says.

"I'm here to—"

"No. First tea, then talk." She pours water from a cast iron kettle into a ceramic teapot and lays a tray of little cakes on the rough wood table. The chairs look to be lashed together from railroad ties, they are so sturdy. I have to wonder how a woman this old can move furniture this large. She perches in the chair across from me.

"I'm not sure I should eat," I say. "I don't really know the laws of this place." And I realize, when I say it, that it's true. I don't know the laws of the heart very well, or don't think I do. I'm an intellectual, a scholar.

And while I love and am loved, I am at—well, heart—a very analytical person.

Or am I?

"The laws of this place are change," she says. "Today it is beautiful. Tomorrow terrible. Today I am old. Tomorrow I shall be young."

"Is there anything that doesn't change here?"

"There's a flame in the middle of the woods. It's ever burning. You could go there and see."

I imagine a lamp on a stick, or a sort of eternal flame like that at some cemeteries.

"If it's not an insult to you, I'd like to go there now. What is your name?" I normally think to ask this earlier.

"They call me Delphi."

On the way out, I realize that "Delphi," in addition to being the name of an oracle, contains an anagram of "phile," a form of the root word in Greek for "love." The D is delta or *daleth*, the letter associated in Qabalah with Venus, the planet of love. I turn to look back, and a beautiful young woman waves goodbye from the door.

I walk for some time, feeling more and more anxious. Finally, I wave down a cart and horse, hoping to ride. "No," the rider tells me. "To get to the fire you have to step off the path."

But I remember that stepping off the path is rarely a good idea when astral traveling. Again, I project a heart toward him. He shimmers and disappears. A deceptive image, then.

The path does lead, eventually, to a series of stone steps spiraling down into a crater in the middle of the forest. At the bottom of the crater, a great mass of magma roils and throws off smoke. This is the eternal fire. It beats with a steady rhythm, as if always on the verge of erupting.

I notice that people have carved petitions into the stone walls of the crater. I use my wand to write the Greek word *Ataraxia* on the wall. Ataraxia is a state of emotional calm and detachment, a thing I aspire toward.

A small man, almost a gnome, appears. "The way to achieve ataraxia is to leap into the fire."

I project a heart on him, but he only grows a little taller.

"I'll be destroyed."

"Only part that changes."

"What doesn't change?" I say. "I'm all parts that change."

He doesn't answer. I debate what to do. The test revealed him consistent with this place, but that doesn't mean he's benign. Good and evil exist even in the astral world. But what he says does describe an initiation ceremony of sorts.

Finally, I fling myself into the caldera. But instead of burning, I fall through it and find myself hovering above the world. I can see Delphi's cottage, as well as the forest and all its creatures. I realize that I have become the sun of this world, shining on it.

I'm not just shining on it: I'm shining in it. I can become a deer in the forest, a tree, even one of the merchants driving carts on the roads. I stream down light and once again take on a body, knowing that I can go back any time. Or, to be more accurate, knowing that I am always there: the real me is a sun always burning over the land of the heart. And the changes of that land are just reflections of my constant light.

I return to my temple by passing through the door once again. I perform a quick banishing ritual, return to my body, and open my physical eyes once again.

This entire experience raises the question: Am I really doing magic or am I simply engaging in some variety of homegrown self-therapy? But more to the point, does it matter? There are undeniable insights in this vision: for example, one doesn't cure worrying by avoiding emotions; one cures it by experiencing the fear one is trying to avoid. Moreover, the idea of achieving ataraxia not by denying emotion but by embracing it is an insight that appeals to me, but doesn't match my preconceptions. It's intriguing. Moreover, I received from this vision information about my own emotional health I did not previously know: for example, the forest is healthy. That's reassuring.

Even if just a sort of self-counseling, what is wrong with that? I grant that we don't want to try to treat serious psychological problems without some professional help, and one shouldn't substitute magic for psychological medication. But meditation and creative visualization can supplement a program of medical treatment.

Two particularly interesting cards to scry are the signifiers. You can approach these as Jungian archetypes, using the one that matches your gender as a way to explore your conscious and using the other to explore your unconscious. Jung asserts that our unconscious mind takes forms of the opposite gender as our own. A man, therefore, who identifies as male has an anima, a female unconscious who may take many forms. Similarly, a woman has an animus, a male unconscious. We can scry this image and speak to the person we discover to open up communication with our unconscious.

The power of this magical approach is that the cards become a two-way system of communication, and just as with any language or system of communication, we need to experiment and make use of it ourselves before we can become fluent. There's a lot of room to move in the Lenormand. A lot of unclaimed territory still lies unexplored.

Keys of Cardboard

The whole idea that we can, by manipulating some pieces of cardboard, create knowledge where there was none previously raises such interesting questions—of knowledge, being, even morality—that I itched to address them.

I know, however, that my skills have rarely risen beyond the ability to pose the questions. A book, like this one, has a conclusion; it has a fixed end, which you are reading now. But I've heard of the tarot also being called a book. If so, it is an older style of book, a set of loose leafs "bound" in a case or box and taken out, one at a time, read, and put back in the same order. But when those leafs go out of order, as they do in the tarot or in a deck of playing cards or in the Lenormand, it's hard to make an argument for any particular leaf being the beginning or end. Yes, we might begin with 1–Rider and end with 36–Cross; we might start with 0–The Fool and end with XXI–The World. But these orders are temporary, contingent. Once shuffled, any deck becomes a new book with a new order.

For me, then, to arrive at solid conclusions about cartomancy would be to impose order on something whose great power and virtue lies in its very disorder. Turn 36–Cross over, and under it again is 1–Rider. Look behind the wreath in which the hermaphrodite dances, and the fool is dangling his foot off a precipice.

We must, in studying these cardboard keys, always keep in mind that we begin where we end. We tread the same ground, in a different order. Cartomancy is waltzing with the concept of significance. For me to say what it all means would be arrogant.

So if you wish to use these keys to open doors in your mind, you must use them. You cannot merely read about them, any more than you can learn to play Bach by reading music theory alone. It will help to read the theory, but ultimately music—and cartomancy—is about the practice.

Appendix I

Okay, Fine, a List of Meanings for the Cards, if You Insist

I relegate this chapter to the hinterland of the appendices because it is, in one important sense, unnecessary, even harmful, to create formulaic interpretations of the Lenormand cards. Yet I'm aware that some readers will insist on it, and for those who wish to use this book to learn to read the cards, a list of such meanings might be of some use for inspiration, rather than formulaic cut-and-paste interpretations.

To that end, and in keeping with the purpose and spirit of this book, these are essentially meditations rather than meanings. They're also personal: they're my meanings, gleaned from several sources and my own experiences with the cards. You will create your own meanings with experience. Having a section like this does give me an excuse to provide some historical context, which I do with all the historical method and skill of a student of literature and not of history.

Which is to say, I probably make more than a few historical errors, despite my best efforts.

So take this section in that spirit, Dear Reader (as an eighteenth-century writer might say), and with a sense of playfulness rather than dogma. If anyone dares say, "Well, Dunn says this card means … " I shall be very, very grumpy.

1. Rider

Imagine you live in the early nineteenth century for a moment. If you want to have an extended conversation with someone, they need to come to you or you need to go to them. Moreover, the fastest you've ever traveled is about 25 miles per hour. A visitor, therefore, is a big deal, but it's also a common occurrence. Anyone who has come to see you has done so at some personal difficulty, but they also do so on a daily basis, without giving it much thought.

That's the tension of the Rider, who represents a visitor or messenger. In our modern world, the Rider is coming a short distance, perhaps on a bike. This is the neighbor who brings you over a casserole when you're feeling ill. It's the friend who drops by for coffee. And, of course, if you're reading for a querent, it may be you or the querent: whichever one of you is the visitor in the other's home.

I feel obligated to point out the obligation of visitors. Showing up at someone's house means you're subject to our society's unwritten hospitality laws, which are strict and unspoken. The guest must bring something as tribute, and must not impose upon the host; the host, in turn, must provide anything the guest needs without quibble or stinginess. This is the card that invokes that hospitality.

The Rider also offers a bit of a threat: the words for "guest" and "host" are actually related to each other etymologically, and both are related to our word "hostile." So look at the cards surrounding the Rider to find his or her attitude.

The cards after the Rider sometimes indicate what the Rider brings: Flowers are gifts, Letters are—letters. Birds are conversation or news. What about the Whip? Pain, perhaps, but also perhaps other kinds of exertion. (Ahem.) The cards following might also indicate what kind of visitor it is to be: a Tree might indicate a family member. Dog is a friend. Bear might indicate a person in power over you: time to impress the boss with your cooking.

2. Clover

The clover in my yard has nearly choked out the witchgrass and creeping charlie. And good thing, too: clover is easy to care for. It's no work at all, and it's pretty and pleasant. This is the card of "ahh, nice, I didn't expect that." We tend to think of clovers as lucky tokens, and this is a lucky card. Everything here is coming up clover.

This card is about things that are easy, lucky, and pleasant.

The shamrock, a particular species of clover, is a symbol of Ireland because St. Patrick, the patron saint of Ireland, used it as a symbol of the trinity. Therefore, this symbol can represent things that come in threes. In the right combination, it might talk about two becoming three, as when a couple has a child.

Sometimes the card in combination reveals the sort of lucky stroke we can expect. If followed by Bear, it might be a windfall. If you're a creative person, and it's followed by Star, it might well indicate a sudden burst of inspiration.

3. Ship

Again, in the nineteenth century, if you wanted to go for any worthwhile trip, you needed something a bit faster and more comfortable than a horse. This was the ship. Now, of course, we have landships in the shape of cars, and airships in the shape of airplanes. This card can mean "long-distance travel." If you couldn't walk there or take a bike, this trip is one represented by Ship.

Some systems put commerce here, but I only read it this way if the commerce specifically involves shipping.

Ships involved some degree of risk, of course, from pirates, storms, and just plain bad luck. Our long-distance travel is a lot safer than it once was, but sometimes this card, if followed by something worrying like Mice or Cross, might indicate travel difficulties: a flat tire, a speeding ticket, or worse. When this card follows a person card, it often indicates a foreigner or someone from far away.

Because long trips often throw us in with strangers, this card can indicate the unknown or distant, especially in more philosophical readings.

In a day-to-day reading, it's just the far away. The cards after sometimes indicate what kind of trip or the destination. Home is a return trip. Birds can indicate air travel. Flowers is a vacation, while Fox might be a business trip.

4. House

Even the birds have their nests to come home to. This card is the place you lay your head at night. It's also everything you keep at home: your family, your things, and sometimes your investments.

Metaphorically, we used to refer to a person's family as their house. This card still means that, as well: your immediate family lives here. When followed by happy cards, like Flowers, this means a happy family. When followed by Scythe, it might mean a break with family: sometimes just an argument, sometimes divorce.

This card is also a person card, and thus can represent a man: usually a father, if not the querent's father. Here combinations become tricky: if followed by Cross, does this mean an unhappy family, or a priest (a "father" of the cross)? And this is exactly why I don't think a list of formulaic meanings will do you much good: in a real reading, context will make it abundantly clear how you read this combination, and intuition must feed into that. You can't write intuition.

5. Tree

Our feet are roots, our spine is a trunk, and our hands and head are branches. The tree is the body itself.

Our body comes from our ancestors, and we speak of "family trees." Where House is the family you live with or near, the Tree is our ancestors. And, of course, the oldest human spiritual system is reverence of ancestors, so this card can also indicate that kind of spirituality.

Giving a health reading is usually a bad idea, for several reasons. If someone substitutes cartomancy for health care, they're making a pretty poor decision. Also, if you predict disaster and are wrong, you'll make someone panic without any good reason; and if you give an "all clear" to someone who really should see a doctor, you could be in serious legal trouble. On the other hand, if reading for yourself how long it'll take for the medicine to start working or for the bone to knit, and you've already gone to a doctor and just want to know, there's no harm in doing a reading with Tree as a signifier for health.

In traditional systems of reading, sometimes Tree was regarded as a negative card when it occurred close to the signifier. I don't use this method of interpretation, but some people still do. I see Tree, like Ship, as a neutral card. Followed by something pleasant, like Clover or Flowers, it means health and physical beauty. Followed by Mice, it might mean a minor or annoying health problem. Followed by Mountain, it can indicate blockages. If followed by Cross, it could be something more serious.

Some people like to read with Tree representing karma, an extension of the "family tree" meaning, with the idea that our karma is a result of our family as well as our past. Here's one of those times when you decide before a reading that you want to read it that way: you just tell yourself, this question involves fate and karma. Tree will represent that part of the question in this reading.

6. Clouds

Where did I put my pen? Wait, what time is it? How did I forget to eat lunch? And have I been wearing this shirt inside-out all day?

Clouds is confusion and obscurity. When it appears in a reading, it's a big shrug.

Some cards, in traditional styles of reading, are read according to their orientation. If you notice, this card in your deck probably has a dark cloud on one side, and a light cloud on the other. Traditionally, those cards on the dark side represent things that are obscured or confused, while those on the other side represent things clearing up. If House is on the dark side, for example, it might mean there's a secret someone in your family is keeping. If House is on the light side, it might mean the lifting of a dark cloud at your house.

You'll notice that Clouds is a person card, the King of Clubs. As usual, clubs are a bit negative: this isn't necessarily a happy person. Perhaps it's someone whose mind is confused, or someone who likes to confuse others. If this is followed by Snake, I might even think of a con man. If it's followed by Lily, I'd imagine it's an older person who has suffered some loss of cognitive abilities.

When Clouds is paired with Fox, it can mean confusion and disorder at work. If Bear, better check your account books. If paired with Tower, I tend to think bureaucracy and endless forms. If it's close to April, I think "taxes."

7. Snake

I rather like snakes. Growing up, we had a massive bull snake that ate mice in the barn. We left it alone, and of course it left us alone. But I also learned a healthy respect: bull snakes are peaceful, and garter snakes are nearly harmless, but even they can nip. We've also got rattlesnakes out in rural Illinois, and a couple times I'd hear a dry shuffle and whisper and decide to walk in a different part of the farm that day.

In the Lenormand, though, Snake is something you don't turn your back on, no matter how peaceful the breed. This is the card of betrayal, sniping, poison, and complexity. Sometimes, Snake just means a tangle; other times, it might mean sarcasm or biting wit. And sometimes it means a devious person.

At the same time, not all devious people are bad. Some might even be allies, as long as you remember that their goal isn't necessarily to be your friend.

Obviously, there's a biblical parallel here, with the most subtle beast of the Garden of Eden offering Eve the apple that caused all the trouble (or all the fun, if you think the Garden sounded kind of dull). Temptation might show up as the Snake, even for those who don't necessarily believe this story. Unfair to the poor snakes, perhaps, but there it is.

This is also a person card: here, a woman, usually a bit older, or perhaps with a devious personality.

8. Coffin

It amuses me slightly that this card, which seems pretty grim, actually isn't all that bad, while Cross, which seems nice enough, is often pretty grim. It almost exactly parallels the general perception of XIII– Death in the tarot. And, in fact, Coffin shares a lot of meaning with that card: it means endings, completion, being boxed up. So having it followed by House might mean a death in the family, but it might just mean boxing up your stuff to move out. In general, *don't* predict death: you'll be wrong most of the time. And if you're reading for yourself, you'll be right only once.

Endings are a kind of change, and so Coffin can mean things are changing. After all, life goes on.

In the nineteenth century, it was common to set out the coffin for viewing in the deceased's home rather than a funeral parlor. In fact, some nineteenth-century homes would have a family coffin they'd store in the attic and trot out during deaths for such an occurrence. After the viewing, the deceased would be placed in a less expensive coffin for burial. Some very old houses have nooks at the staircase landings, so that one could position the coffin down the stairs. None of this has anything to do with the meaning of the card, but is really interesting.

232 • *Appendix I*

9. Bouquet or Flowers

Flowers are the sexual organs of plants. Fruit is a plant's ovaries. Next time you eat an apple, remember: you're crunching into a delicious tree ovary, and the next time you smell a rose, you're sticking your nose in the genitals of a plant.

Strangely, however, this card isn't really sexual: instead, it's a card of innocent fun and beauty. It's the card of art. Followed by Star, it might be music, or just a beautiful mind. It's also the card of gifts, of course, and decorations. Followed by Tree, it might represent makeup or other efforts at personal beautification. Followed by the Sun, it's stunning beauty. Followed by the Moon, it might be a celebrity.

This, too, is a person card: here, usually a young, pretty woman, innocent and perhaps flighty.

There's also the tradition of tossing the bouquet at weddings. This derives from a number of old traditions of the bride offering gifts to the wedding party, including bits of her own clothing. The idea here is surrendering what you once had and will never need again: the gown you were married in, the flowers that decorated your innocence, and so on. The tradition evolved to a toss and the idea that whoever got the bouquet would be the next to marry. This card can indicate marriage or availability. If it follows another person card, it could mean that person is attractive, but it could also mean they're single.

10. Scythe

This the card of abrupt endings. If you were to dig through eighteenth and nineteenth century poetry, you'd find scythes mentioned often. They're symbols of time, of ending, of harvest, and of sudden death. The swift and irreversible action of the scythe also makes it a card of choices with no going back.

In the European tradition, the Scythe is often interpreted as "cutting" the card on the side of the blade (usually the right side). So when followed by Mountain, it means "cutting through a delay." When followed by Cross or Mice, it might mean "cutting through worry or annoyances." Followed by Anchor, it may mean a sudden change of lifestyle, or a "coming unmoored."

I tend to lump everything sharp and pokey in with this card. It's surgery, sculpting, and even cooking if the context supports those interpretations.

11. Whip, Birch, or Broom

Whack!

We live now in a time, mercifully, when we no longer regard it as a civilized or helpful act to beat children with rods. And, thank goodness, it's no longer a given that a husband should, from time to time, smack his wife. In fact, it's reprehensible.

And yet we're still knocked about by other kinds of birches and brooms. This is the card of a good drubbing, either physically or, more often for the lifestyle most of us lead, metaphorically. Even verbal arguments (especially if followed by Birds) show up here, and punishment of an official nature might be indicated if followed by Tower or Book.

At the same time, because we used to regard—quite wrongly—physical reinforcement as essential to discipline, this card can also mean acts that take a lot of discipline. If you're asking about your violin performance, this card might represent practice. If you're an athlete, it represents exertion of all types, as well as exercise.

In fact, there's one type of exercise that Sylvie Steinbach associates with this card specifically: sexual exercise. I don't think she's making a joke about sadomasochism here: it's just that the line between pain and pleasure is a fuzzy one, as any marathon runner can tell you.

12. Birds or Owls

Here we have two birds singing to each other. Most birdsong, incidentally, is either establishing territory or inviting a mate. Those beautiful songs boil down to "Hey, I'm available" or "My tree! Back off!" Human conversation, on a day-to-day basis, is often pretty similar: it's mostly grooming behavior. "Good morning, how are you?" is really saying "I am friendly to you." Well, it beats eating each other's lice, which is what our primate cousins do instead.

This card therefore indicates conversation, or less politely, gossip. It is one of several cards of communication, but where Letter is written communication, this card represents spoken communication or rumor.

The card after it often indicates the subject or quality of the conversation. Whip indicates oneupmanship, or argument. Followed by House, it's a family meeting. Followed by Fox, it's workplace conversation. And followed by Cross, it's bad news. If followed by Garden, it's a group conversation.

Traditionally this card has also referred to things that come in pairs. So if you see it near Child, it might indicate twins if the context supports it. And if asking a question about time, it might mean two days, weeks, months, or years.

13. Child

Obviously, this card represents children. But I know a lot of people who refer to their pets as their children, and I often think of my books as children. By extension, then, this card represents anything small that requires our care.

The entire idea of children was a new one to the nineteenth century, which might be a hard thing for us to understand. We assume that there's a natural category of "child," but in reality for much of Western history, children were seen as merely small and underdeveloped adults. The child labor of the eighteenth century was a purely practical concern. After all, children were agile and had small hands, very useful for all sorts of work. It was only as the idea that children possessed a valuable quality of innocence grew that putting them to work began to seem regrettable.

The nineteenth century is also the time we began to understand that children learned in a way different from adults. Even our technical term, *pedagogy*, means "leading children." This card, then, can also mean education.

The cards that follow this one might give us an indication of what kind of child it is. Followed by a work-related card, like Book or Fox, it could just indicate a new project. Followed by Tower, it can indicate a school or school system. When this card follows other cards, it often means "a little" or "small." For example, Ship followed by Child could mean a short trip.

14. Fox

Fox is an interesting card from a historical perspective, because it's one of those cards whose meaning differs a lot from tradition to tradition. In some traditions, it indicates an enemy or betrayal. But in others, it's a sign of cleverness. And a lot of American readers, following Sylvie Steinbach, use it as the chief indicator of work.

Why is a fox on a card at all? Why not any number of other animals? Because the fox is symbolically important to a particular subset of European culture, in the form of the fox hunt. This diversion, often engaged in by both men and women, involved letting a fox out of a cage and giving it a small head-start, then releasing dogs and chasing after them on horseback. I suspect, due to the mixed genders and general chaos possible in this sport, it served as an excuse to steal a few moments with a member of the opposite sex without a chaperone around. One could always claim that one's dogs followed the wrong trail, perhaps that of a wild goose.

Foxes were chosen for this sport because they were small, fast, and clever enough to make it a challenge for the dogs. Hence, we get the notion of cleverness out of this sport. But foxes also were predators that attacked chickens and other small farm animals. Having a fox steal your best laying hen was no doubt a frustrating experience, which might account for the symbolism of enmity.

How, then, did it come to mean "work" for some? I don't know exactly, but it seems to be an extension of the idea that foxes are particularly clever and most of us work at jobs that require more cleverness than other traits. Even those performing physical labor need to think fast on the job; we live in a time when intelligence and quick wits are well-rewarded.

I usually read this card as cleverness and short-term jobs or projects. The card that follows may indicate the kind of job: a Cross might mean a priest or religious vocation, a Book might indicate a writer or scholar, and a Tower is a government job. When this card follows a person card, it either shows that the querent knows him or her from work, or that he or she is particularly clever—although not always in the querent's favor.

15. Bear

This big fellow is a symbol of power and force for the typical European, partially because of the sport of bear hunting and partially because of the regrettable pastime of bear-baiting, in which a bear bound by a chain is set upon by several dogs, and spectators place bets on which dog will eventually kill it. This latter tradition was popular around Shakespeare's time, so by the time the Lenormand was invented it was mostly a memory. But it's worth keeping in mind that in the background of this card is the idea that the big and powerful can be brought down by the small and vicious.

This card indicates two qualities of the bear at the same time. First, it shows the power of the bear: it can often represent a boss or authority figure, particularly an intimidating one. Second, it recalls the bear's ravenous behavior before it goes to sleep for the winter. This card can represent, therefore, what and how we eat, as well as how we get our food. By extension, then, some people read this card as the card of money and income.

That's a lot for one card to bear.

16. Stars

If you've never been outside of a city, you've never really seen the stars. Take a drive out to the country some night, turn off the lights of your car, and sit in the dark for a few minutes. Then you'll see that the night sky is filled with light. Looking up at these stars makes one think—and that, perhaps, is one of the reasons this card represents the mind. At the same time, it indicates success in endeavor and even "star quality" or creativity. It's a very all-purpose, positive card.

When it represents the mind, followed by Cross it can indicate a troubled or depressed mind. Followed by Mice, an anxious mind. Followed by Bear it can mean that you have money on your mind, and followed by Book it can indicate creativity, literary or otherwise.

Because of its association with the pentagram, a symbol representing occult tradition, Stars can also indicate an interest in esoteric matters. When it follows a person card, it may indicate such an interest, and when I see it after Book, in my profession, I know it's probably talking about a book on magic or the occult.

The Star can also indicate a goal or aspiration, especially if the context suggests it.

17. Storks

The Storks are a sign of change, almost always for the better. Storks are migratory birds, so they often indicate a change or move of home. Of course, in modern mythology, we pretend that children are brought by storks, so they can also indicate that kind of change. But in general, they are an improvement in place or circumstances.

The cards following the Storks indicate the type of change. If House, it's probably a move. If Child, a child. If Ring, an engagement. If Ship, perhaps a long-term trip or a new car. If Letter or Bear, a possible pay raise or promotion.

This is a person card, at least technically. It might indicate a tall, mercurial person, although in my experience it rarely does. Perhaps I just don't have many such people in my life.

18. Dog

Dogs were among the first animals humans domesticated. Through generations of selective breeding from their wolf ancestors, we've created a species of animal that is intelligent enough to work and play by our side. The dog has long been a symbol of loyal service, even when one's hounds were work animals and not loving pets. The dog's intelligence elevates it to the status of near-human, which is why many cultures have a taboo against eating dogs (and those cultures that do eat dog usually only eat specific breeds that are never raised as pets).

Dog sometimes does just stand for a pet, but it can also indicate a human friend. When it occurs next to a person card, it usually indicates that the person is familiar to the querent, even if not a friend. Some readers use Dog to represent the partner in a gay relationship.

When Dog stands for a friend, the card after it can indicate what kind of friend or what that friend does for the querent. If it's Snake, it might be a devious or two-faced friend. If Cross, a counselor or spiritual partner. If Lily, an older friend or mentor. If Ship, a distant friend or a travel companion.

19. Tower

If you read the tarot, do not panic. This isn't the same kind of Tower as in the tarot card of the same name, although it shares some similarities. This Tower is a watchtower or fortress tower, and represents authority, power, and public buildings of all types.

It can indicate schools, universities, courthouses, and by extension higher education, law, and government. It can also indicate anything metaphorically lofty or high or far-seeing. This card heavily depends on context. In questions about a dispute, it probably means recourse to official arbitration or the courts. In questions about love, though, it might indicate a courthouse where a marriage might occur, or if followed by Cross, a church or other religious building.

Metaphorically, it can also stand for perspective and "rising above it all."

The cards after it can indicate the type of building, if it is indeed a building. Book will indicate a school, university, or library. Letter will indicate a post office. Ship, a foreign corporation or travel agent or embassy. Lily might indicate a museum, and so on.

20. Garden

What do you do when you'd like to have people over, but your house is just too small—or too messy? Simple: you have a cookout and eat in the yard. Some things rarely change, so Garden indicates public or semipublic gatherings. It's the party card, whether a dinner party or a potluck.

But the garden also had philosophical meaning to the Romantic imagination. For one thing, it was a place where the creative power of nature met the creative genius of the individual: we could shape nature into our own image. Voltaire's *Candide*, for example, ends with the exhortation that we should "cultivate our garden." This precept, in distinction to the optimism of Pangloss, is simultaneously a reminder that nature is beautiful, including human nature, but it requires cultivation. One cannot simply trust that a garden will grow out of the tilled soil.

So in a more philosophical reading, this card can represent cultivated human nature. In most readings, of course, it will stand for social interaction, and the card after it will describe the kind of interaction. If followed by Moon, it'll be a party with lots of big names. If it's followed by Fox, it might be a salon or a work party. If followed by Snake, I'd RSVP my regrets.

21. Mountain

Mountains have always indicated solitude and meditation in the West. Moses' encounter with God the Lawgiver took place on a mountain, and in the popular culture we have the image of the wise man sitting, meditating, on the peak of a mountain. We also have the odd and expensive (and thoroughly Romantic!) sport of mountain climbing, in which individuals brave great hardship and difficulty in order to scale a giant rock—"because it's there."

In a reading, Mountain means a challenge or an obstacle. It often indicates a delay—something you have to go around or climb at great effort. For some people, this notion of a challenge is a source of excitement. Others would rather not have to deal with it.

The card after Mountain indicates the kind of delay or obstacle. If Ship follows it, plan for a delayed flight. If Bear follows it, it might be a blockage in your income. If Fish follows it and you're asking about a financial venture, it might not be the best investment. If Ring follows it, expect a delayed contract or wedding.

Mountain can also indicate, as I said, challenge or blockage. When it follows Tree, it can indicate a physical or spiritual blockage (Tree + Mountain is the combination indicating constipation. Now you know. If nothing else, you've got your money's worth in that tidbit of knowledge). Star followed by Mountain might indicate an *idee fixe*, an obsessive thought.

22. Crossroads

The folklore of crossroads stretches back to ancient Greece, where the goddess Hekate guards the meeting of roads, and where statues of Hermes, called Herms, were erected at crossroads. In Rome, you had Trivia, a goddess of the Three Ways, and in later Europe you had a tradition of using crossroads as a place of public execution. Due to all this they became associated with magic, and in American folklore that's where you meet the devil to learn to play the guitar.

In the Lenormand, the card usually means a choice, a fork in the road literal or metaphorical. The card or two after it may indicate the nature of the choices.

But keep in mind, especially in more esoteric readings, the ancient folklore of this important site. Also, since this is a person card, we can get some clues as the kind of person we're facing. We're facing the Queen of Diamonds, but she's Hekate or Trivia here. She offers a choice, but she's dark, mysterious, and perhaps a master of occult knowledge.

When this card follows another, it might mean "multiple." Children + Crossroads might mean many children. Mountain + Crossroads might mean myriad delays.

23. Mice

The poet Robert Burns assures the little mouse he has found in his field that "a daimen icker in a thrave/'S a sma' request"—which is to say, a single ear of grain in a bundle of twenty-four isn't too big of a request for a mouse to make from the farmer. But a mouse can eat a heck of a lot more than a daimen icker in a thrave. They can eat the whole thrave, and then foul the rest of the bundles with their feces. When Mouse turns up in a reading, then, it represents loss, theft, and annoyances.

Yet a mouse is a small annoyance, and can be dealt with. This isn't a card of disaster, usually. It can indicate theft, but in my experience it most often indicates lost objects, annoying breakdowns and failures, and unexpected maintenance costs. When it shows up after House, it can actually signify vermin of some type, or small but urgent repairs. If it follows Anchor, it can mean a plumbing problem, or a dissolute lifestyle, depending on context. If it follows Ship, take your car in for a tune-up, and if it follows Tree, make an appointment with your GP for a checkup.

When I see this card, I tend to think "annoying." It can also mean "busy, but to no avail," especially if following Fox. If it follows a person card, it might indicate that the person thus represented is potentially dishonest in a petty way.

24. Heart

The symbol of the heart is a mysterious one. It looks nothing like a human heart at all, so what is it originally? One suggestion is that it is a pair of inverted testicles, which I suppose it could be. The other possibility is that it a pair of buttocks and the vulva. That seems more likely to me. In any event, this is a symbol whose innocence may hide a less innocent origin.

In the Lenormand, this card indicates emotions, usually positive ones although not necessarily. It can also point to courage, as the word *courage* comes from the same root as the French word for "heart."

The cards that follow this one indicate the kind of emotion. If it is followed by Stars, Moon, Sun, and other positive cards, it is usually love or happiness. If it's followed by Clouds, it is a broken heart, confusion, or sadness. If followed by Mountain, it may indicate unrequited love. If followed by Whip, it could indicate sexual attraction.

When this card follows a person card, it signifies an emotional connection, usually love-related. Notice it does not indicate a relationship, necessarily, just the emotion. When I see Heart and Snake, it's hard not to think of infidelity.

25. Ring

In Anglo-Saxon society, a lord would buy his thegns' loyalty by offering them gifts, often gold arm rings. Thus, he is sometimes called the Ring-Giver. Such a gift created a contract between the lord and his thegns: he would provide for them, and in return they would protect him and his lands. The wedding ring in modern culture is a similar contract, although the lines of power are—hopefully—less unequal.

Since most querents will only get married a few times (usually in a row), it makes sense to extend the meaning of Ring out from marriage into any kind of contract. After all, most nineteenth-century women had few business prospects outside of marriage. But modern querents probably enter into many contracts in their day-to-day lives.

The card following Ring will indicate the type of contract. Ring + Snake will indicate an unfair or deceptive contract, while Ring + Fish is a business contract, potentially lucrative. Ring + Heart is a clear sign of marriage.

When Ring is close to a person card, it indicates that the querent is in a contract with that person, perhaps that of marriage itself.

26. Book

For bibliophiles like myself, Book is a pleasant card. It can indeed represent an actual physical book, particularly if the context warrants it. For writers, it is the logical signifier for the current writing project. For others, it has a range of metaphorical meanings.

For one thing, it can indicate secrets, as if it were a locked diary hidden away somewhere. It can also indicate the abstract idea of scholarship itself. And it sometimes represents the memory.

When followed by Snake, it can indicate a faulty memory or dangerous secret. When followed by House, it might represent household accounts. Followed by Star, it could indicate a book of poetry, and followed by Moon it may even be a bestseller. That's a combination I've never seen in my own personal readings, sad to say.

Book can also indicate the occult, because of the study involved in it. This interpretation links it, again, to secrets.

27. Letter

I've written elsewhere about the vital importance of letters as a means of communication to homebound eighteenth- and nineteenth-century women. The very first novels of the eighteenth century, in fact, are epistolary, or in letter form, because their authors could not imagine a story not told in letters. Until very recently, the post office in England delivered the mail several times a day (at one point, apparently, mail arrived in the city six times every day!). And one of the earliest and most important offices established in the early American colonies was the post office. We forget the importance of letters, perhaps, because we receive so few of them.

On the other hand, we do receive written communications: emails, texts, even blog posts. These pieces of writing are also represented by the card Letter.

Letter can also represent paperwork in general. The cards following it give either the content of the letter, or the nature of the paperwork.

For example, if Letter is followed by Mountain, it's a delayed letter. If followed by House, it's home-related paperwork. If followed by Bear, it's a bill, while Heart or Dog indicates a more friendly, personal communication.

28. Gentleman

This card represents the querent if male. Otherwise, it represents the most important man in the querent's life.

29. Lady

This card represents a female querent or the most important woman in the querent's life. In my experience, these genders are fluid: do not assume that Lady always represents a woman. Sometimes I think these cards should be renamed Self and Other, leaving gender out of it. But gender was of vital importance to the nineteenth century—it was destiny.

30. Lily

This card displays a wide variety of meanings, from sexuality to spiritual peace. You can almost identify the tradition of Lenormand reader by his or her meaning of this card. In Europe, it often means sexuality or pleasure. In America, especially among those who ascribe sexuality to the Whip, it is a symbol of peace, satisfaction, completion, and age.

Being a person card, it can indicate an older man (or woman), often a mentor or sage figure.

When Lily follows a card representing a physical object, I like to think of it as meaning something like "old" or "venerable." So Book + Lily might mean an old book, and Ship + Lily might mean an antique car, if such a meaning is appropriate to the context. At other times, I take Lily to mean "peaceful," so when it follows a negative card I read it as the wisdom to deal with the problem represented. For example, Cross + Lily implies worry and difficulties overcome through wisdom and serenity.

31. Sun

This card is one of those confluences of meaning between the Lenormand and the tarot. It has almost the same range of meanings as the tarot's Sun. Many contemporary readers take a psychological approach, using Sun to indicate the outward ego. It's a card of warmth, happiness, and joy.

Often, it can be read literally. If asking when something will occur, for example, Sun could indicate "during the day." When Sun follows another card, I try to read it as "bright" or "warm." So Lily + Sun might be an older mentor figure who is warm toward the querent.

A few particular combinations indicate some unambiguous meanings. When Sun is on the lighter side of the Clouds, it indicates the sun breaking out from behind clouds; the opposite, of course, is relevant when it is on the darker side. Similarly, Snake + Sun means a deception coming to light.

32. Moon

Moon indicates the inner life of the querent, the intuition and, for some querents, the spiritual side of life. Literally, it can indicate that something happens at night (ignoring the inconvenient fact that the moon is visible during the day for much of its cycle). It can also signify dreams, both in the literal sense and in the sense of goals for the future.

Traditionally, the moon can indicate fame, because it's the light reflected from the sun. We can extend that meaning to reputation, as well, for those querents concerned about such things.

The Moon, appropriately, has a double nature: it's both the inner life of the querent and the reflected outer life. It can also, then, represent cyclic changes. So reading this card requires—appropriately—more intuition than usual.

When I read it in combination, I usually link it to the context more than other cards. For example, in Cross + Moon it could be troubling dreams, if that seems relevant, or worries about reputation, or Wiccan spirituality. Heart + Moon could be an inconstant heart, but it could also be a yearning for fame.

33. Key

After Moon, it's nice to see a card with a clear and unambiguous meaning. Key means "yes." When it follows any card, it acts as an exclamation point. It can be a card of opening, destiny, and so forth, but you'll rarely go wrong if you just look at the card it follows and say, "Yeah, that, again." If it follows Ring, expect a marriage or contract, without a doubt. If it follows a person card, that person is extremely important: pay attention to them.

The only complexity is that Key is usually positive, so when it follows a negative card or combination, it indicates "a way out." So Cross + Key could be "intense worry" but is more likely to be "a way out of your burdens." Look at the following card for the nature of that key. If it's a person card, consider that it might be outside help. If it's Ship, it could be a literal or figurative putting of distance between oneself and a problem.

34. Fish

The little fishies in the pond all swim where they will. This card, therefore, indicates independence, freedom, and fluency.

Where Fox indicates work or a job, Fish can represent a career or a businessperson who creates his or her own money. In fact, since it's a person card, Fish can literally mean "a big fish," a mover and shaker.

Fish is a card of capitalism. When it indicates a business, the card following can show the kind of business. Fish + Tower is a major corporation, while Fish + Child is the childcare industry, Fish + Bear is the food industry, and Fish + Book is the educational or publishing sector.

35. Anchor

This has always struck me as a strange symbol for a divination system. It's a bit like a Brake Pads card. But so it goes: sometimes we move ahead like the Ship, and sometimes we drop Anchor and stop.

But we already have a card that indicates stopping and delay: Mountains.

The difference, of course, is that we can't control where the mountains are, but we can control when we drop anchor. So Anchor is where we choose to stop, physically and metaphorically. Anchor, therefore, can be the card of rest. Metaphorically, where we stop and rest is our lifestyle, our way of living. For example, if you're doing a reading about someone wishing to change jobs and Anchor comes up, you might start asking the person what it is about their lifestyle they don't want to change.

The cards after Anchor can indicate the kind of lifestyle we're discussing. If it's followed by House, it's a nice domestic life, with or without picket fences. If followed by Ship, it's a traveling and vagrant lifestyle, and if it's followed by Moon we might be dealing with a bohemian of some variety.

36. Cross

This card is not the happiest card in the deck; in fact, in my opinion, it's the least happy. But like many cards, it has two meanings. On its basic level, it means religion, and not just Christianity. But since people often turn to religion in times of trouble, it can also mean trouble, especially worry and grief. Read this card carefully.

When it indicates religion, such as when you're trying to learn about someone you don't know, the card after it can give a hint as to the kind of religion. Cross + Star can indicate Judaism or Paganism, depending on context. Cross + Book can indicate a holy text, or one of the religions of the book, while Cross + Moon can indicate Islam or Wicca, again depending on context.

More often, though, it indicates something that sends us to prayer: a problem. Even in reading atheists and agnostics, the card can be read as a concern or burden. After all, the cross was a symbol long before Jesus was hung on it, and it wasn't a particularly pleasant symbol for anyone. The symbol of Christianity is, for better or worse, a tool of torture. Remember that "excruciating" has the word *crux* in it, meaning "cross."

And, of course, cross can also mean crux, in the sense of an important event that determines our future direction—especially when near Crossroads. Often, those events feel unpleasant at the time, but we later look back and think, "Ah, without that I wouldn't be who I am now."

The card following Cross can indicate the nature, and sometimes the way out of, the worry. Cross + Coffin is grief over an ending. Cross + Heart is a broken heart. But when Cross is followed by a very positive card, like Key, or when it is on the lighter side of Clouds, it can indicate a passing out of or escaping from grief.

Appendix Two

Lenormand Keyword Table

	Things	People	Descriptions	Places
1–Rider	Means of short-distance travel; **Message**	Messenger Athlete Visitor	**Athletic;** Swift, Active **Distant** (but usually within neighborhood)	Garages, Car dealerships
2–Clover	Games	Gambler	**Lucky, Unexpected.**	Casinos
3–Ship	Means of long-distance travel	Foreigner	**Far away (usually outside of local zip code); foreign;** exotic	Ships, bodies of water

*These cards sometimes directly indicate people, while other cards describe people only in combinations with those cards.

Bolded keywords are the most common meanings in most readings.

	Things	People	Descriptions	Places
4–House	House, Private building	*Family Parents Landlord	Solid; Stable	Home
5–Tree	Body; **Health**	Doctor Nurse Therapist	Healthy Strong	Forests
6–Clouds	**Confusion**	*Older man, somewhat untrustworthy.	**Murky. Uncertain.**	Unknown places. Hiding places.
7–Snake	**Deception;** Betrayal	*Older woman.	**Untrustworthy** Dishonest Convoluted	Places where illegal or immoral activity occurs
8–Coffin	**Conclusions** Box; Container **Transformation**	Mortician Coroner Ancestor	**Concluded Contained**	Funeral homes Cemeteries Storage areas Basements
9–Flowers	**Gift** Trinket	*Younger woman Artist	**Beautiful Pleasant Lovely** Young	Beauty parlor; Art museum, gallery, or studio
10–Scythe	**Decision Sudden end** Breakup	Surgeon Ex-partner	**Sudden**	Field Butcher shop Surgery
11–Whip	**Sex** Exertion Exercise Pain	Attractive person; Muscular person	Sexy Sore **Painful**	Gymnasium Basic training
12–Birds	Gossip **Talking** Telephone call	A talker; Know-it-all or busybody	Talkative	Once, social parlor. Now, anywhere one can receive a phone call or visitor

	Things	People	Descriptions	Places
13–Child	New project	*Child	Young New	Nursery
14–Fox	Work, Job	Coworker	Clever, Witty	Workplace Office
15–Bear	Cash flow Food	Boss	Big Strong	Restaurant Boss's office
16–Stars	Success Vision Mind	Visionary Artist or Thinker Occultist.	Occult Mystical	Outside Night
17–Stork	Change Improvement	Remodeler Life coach	Renewed Better	
18–Dog	Loyalty	*Friend Partner	Familiar Known	
19–Tower	Legal matters	Government representative.	Official Public Alone	Public building University Government building
20–Garden	Gathering Party	Neighbors Strangers Gathered people.	Social	Gathering place Party or friendly gathering Park
21–Mountains	Delays Block Obstacle	Hermit	Slow Still Isolated	Distant, isolated, and difficult to access location

	Things	People	Descriptions	Places
22–Crossroads	**Options** Choices	*A woman, usually unmarried	**Many**	Roads, driveways, and paths
23–Mice	Annoyance **Loss Waste** Worry	Thief	**Stressful** Anxious	A job at which much work is done but nothing is ever finished
24–Heart	Happiness **Love**	Lover	**Happy** Joyful Beloved	Boudoir
25–Ring	**Contract** Marriage Agreement	**Spouse;** Partner (personal or legal); A circle of friends	Legal Joined	
26–Book	**Study** Knowledge Secrets; **Memory**	Studious person; Reader or writer	Learned Educated	Library School
27–Letter	**Written message** (includes email and, apparently, text messages) Document Certificate	Postal carrier Graduate	Written	Post office
28–Gentleman		*Male Querent, or Querent's partner	Masculine	

	Things	People	Descriptions	Places
29–Lady		*Female Querent, or Querent's partner.	Feminine	
30–Lily	Peace Satisfaction	*A man	Old Wise	Retirement home
31–Sun	Success Light Personality	Extrovert	Bright Warm	Daytime
32–Moon	Intuition Emotions Fame	Celebrity Introvert Mother	Dreamy Soon Seductive Hidden	Nighttime
33–Key	Tool Attention Karma "Yes"	An important person	Important Destined Fated	
34–Fish	Adventure Independence (esp. financial)	*Entrepreneur Wealthy person	Wealthy Free Independent Adventurous	Water
35–Anchor	Lifestyle Roots	Sailor	Stable Lasting	Beach Hometown
36–Cross	Worry Burden Religion	Religious person or clergy	Heavy Dreary Spiritual	Church or place of worship (any religion) Graveyard

Bibliography

Agrippa, Henry Cornelius. *Three Books of Occult Philosophy.* Ed. Donald Tyson. Woodbury, MN: Llewellyn, 2007.

Bardon, Franz. *Initiation into Hermetics.* Salt Lake City: Merkur Publications, 2005.

Betz, Hans Dieter. *The Greek Magical Papyri in Translation: Including the Demotic Spells.* Chicago: University of Chicago Press, 1992.

Blake, William. *The Portable Blake.* Ed. Alfred Kazin. New York: Viking, 1971.

Brontë, Charlotte. *Jane Eyre.* New York: Random House, 2000.

Bruno, Giordano. *De Magia Mathematica.* http://www .esotericarchives.com/bruno/magiamat.htm (accessed August 13, 2010).

Burkert, Walter. *Greek Religion.* Cambridge: Harvard University Press, 1985.

Cornell, Ann Weiser. *The Power of Focusing: A Practical Guide to Emotional Self-Healing.* Oakland, CA: New Harbinger, 1996.

Decker, Ronald, Thierry Depaulis and Michael Dummett. *A Wicked Pack of Cards: The Origins of the Occult Tarot.* New York: St. Martins Press, 1996.

DuQuette, Lon Milo. *The Book of Ordinary Oracles.* Boston: Weiser, 2005.

English, Jane. "A Scientist's Experience with Tarot." *Wheel of the Tarot: A New Revolution.* Ed. by James Wanless and Angeles Arrien. Carmel, CA: Merrill-West Publishing, 1992.

Ferrer, Juan García. *El Método Lenormand: Todo Sobre las Cartas Lenormand.* Raleigh, NC: Lulu.com, 2008.

Fries, Jan. *Helrunar: A Manual of Rune Magick.* Oxford: Mandrake, 1993.

————. *Seidways: Shaking, Swaying, and Serpent Mysteries.* Oxford: Mandrake, 2009.

Greer, Mary K. *21 Ways to Read a Tarot Card.* Woodbury, MN: Llewellyn, 2007.

Gronow, R. H. *Celebrities of London and Paris.* London: Smith, Elder & Co., 1865.

Jacobs, W. W. "The Monkey's Paw." *Gaslight* (1902). http://gaslight .mtroyal.ca/mnkyspaw.htm (accessed August 13, 2010).

Kraig, Donald Michael. *Tarot & Magic.* St. Paul, MN: Llewellyn, 2003.

Mayer, Elizabeth Lloyd. *Extraordinary Knowing: Science, Skepticism, and the Inexplicable Powers of the Human Mind.* New York: Bantam, 2007.

Pollack, Rachel. *Seventy-Eight Degrees of Wisdom: A Book of Tarot.* San Francisco: Weiser, 1997.

Regardie, Israel. *The Golden Dawn.* St. Paul, MN: Llewellyn, 1989.

Spare, A. O. *The Zöetic Grimoire of Zos.* http://hermetic.com/spare /grimoire_of_zos.html (accessed August 13, 2010).

Steinbach, Sylvie. *The Secrets of the Lenormand Oracle.* Lexington, KY: Booksurge Publishing, 2007.

Tyson, Donald. *Portable Magic: Tarot is the Only Tool You Need.* Woodbury, MN: Llewellyn, 2006.

Wagg, Jeff. "One Million Dollar Paranormal Challenge." The James Randi Educational Foundation. (October 2008). http://www .randi.org/site/index.php/1m-challenge.html (accessed August 13, 2010).

Index